Adapt!

How to Survive and Thrive
In the Changing World of Work

Steve Amos
Charlotte Backman
Rochelle Burgess
John Hall
Michael D. Hardesty
Hal Hendrix
Steve Howard
Joanna Maxwell
Janet L. Newcomb
Lee Pound
James Richards
Jacqueline A. Soares
Krystal Jalene Thomas

Solutions Press
Newport Beach, California

Adapt!
How to Survive and Thrive
In the Changing World of Work

Published by Solutions Press
4533 MacArthur Blvd., #200
Newport Beach, CA 92660

First edition printed March 2009

ISBN: 978-0-975261-7-2

Printed in the United States of America

This is a work of non-fiction. The ideas presented are those of each author alone. All references to possible income to be gained from the techniques discussed in this book relate to specific past examples and are not necessarily representative of any future results specific individuals may achieve.

www.adaptsurviveandthrive.com

Dedication

This book is dedicated to the many people who have touched our lives and to those whose lives we have been privileged to touch and to those who will be touched by this book.

A few of the occupations we've performed ...

Academic Account executive Accounting assistant Actor
Advisor Advocate Appraiser Artist Art teacher Assembler
Author Barmaid Barista Blogger Board member Business
partner Buyer Camera and computer sales Cancer
researcher Career counselor Caretaker CFO Change agent
Childcare worker Coach Commercial appraiser Construction
crew Contract administrator Consultant Copywriter Cytology
technician Darkroom employee Daughter Division governor
Editor Engineer Engineer liaison Entrepreneur
Environmentalist Executive Expert Father Film writer General
dogs body Girl Scout Healer Home remodeler Housekeeper
Housesitter Human Resources professional Husband In-
house counsel Janitor Journalist Lampshade designer
Landlord Lawyer Lead engineer Leader Leasing administrator
Lifeguard Life skills teacher Manager Management consultant
Managing partner Manufacturing engineer Market researcher
Marketing assistant Marketing strategist Massage therapist
Material handler Math tutor Mediator Mentor Mother Mountain
climber Mystery shopper Ombudsman Outplacement
counselor Order administrator Organizational development
specialist Owner Paralegal Pastor Pharmacist President
Problem solver Process engineer Producer Professor Project
manager Quality engineer R&D project engineer Resident
engineer Residential appraiser Restaurant hostess Salesman
Secretary Seller Seminar developer Son Speaker Student
Teacher Telemarketer Therapist Toy developer Trainer
Trouble shooter Vice President Volunteer Waitress Wedding
officiant Wife Writer Camera and Computer Sales
Commercial Appraiser Darkroom Employee Engineer Liaison
Landlord Lifeguard Manufacturing Engineer Material Handler
Math Tutor Quality Engineer President & Janitor Process
Engineer Project Manager Residential Appraiser Salesman

Table of Contents

Section 3: Advanced Career Tactics

Introduction

Have the massive changes taking place today caught you unprepared? Does today's world of work seem like a bizarre caricature of what you expected when you started your career? In a world where jobs have become commodities, are you among the many people asking, "How will I survive?"

Our message to you is, yes, you will survive. You can even learn to thrive in this change filled world of work.

This book was born in a small writer's group hosted by John Hall in Irvine, California. We had no charter to change the world. We simply wanted to improve our writing skills. Our projects were diverse, ranging from articles to marketing materials and book projects.

In such an intimate group, we quickly got to know each other and found that we shared similar career paths and fascinating work experiences, some good; some not-so-good. These experiences made us who we are today. As we quickly discovered, none of us planned in the beginning to end up in our present careers. They evolved naturally. So did this book.

After much trial and error, we realized that our careers, and most successful careers, are based on several powerful insights: Adapt to situations, learn from past triumphs and mistakes, be passionate about what you do, and above all else, be true to yourself.

We didn't intend to write this book. However, as we realized the power these ideas had in our lives, we knew we had to share them. We invited other successful people, who have adapted and thrived, to contribute their stories.

This book will expand your thinking about how to adapt. It collects the experiences and insights of real people - people with different backgrounds, aspirations, careers, and jobs, who struggled with hard questions, found inspiration, made

1

progress, made mistakes, and learned about the world of work and themselves along the way.

In Section One, you will read about our career experiences.

In Section Two, we share wisdom and strategies that will ease your career transitions.

In Section Three, we present advanced strategies that many of us have used successfully.

As you read this book, start to build your self knowledge. Success means different things to different people. Get clear on your definition of success. Is it lots of money? Holding down a prestigious position? Helping others? Discovering a cure for cancer? Once you are clear, ask yourself this question, "How do I get from where I am today to where I want to be?"

Should you change jobs? Find a new profession? Change industries? Go back to school? Start a business? You may not think you need such a drastic change, but industry problems, market conditions, new technologies, management mistakes, competitors, or an unbearable boss may force you onto a new path. Ready or not, sooner or later, change happens.

We've found that many important changes in our lives were not planned. They happened in spite of our plans. As you deal with your life circumstances, remember, you are not alone. While there are no set answers that work for everyone, you will find that, like life, your career is a journey and that you can choose to set the direction.

As you read the following chapters, absorbing the lessons and principles can help you navigate your career journey. Collectively, we have made almost every mistake possible (at least the big ones) and have thrived in spite of, and because of, our experiences. You can too. You always have choices – often more than you realize. Learn from our experiences, then Adapt!

Section One

How We Got Here

"Nothing is a waste of time if you use the experience wisely."

Auguste Rodin
1840-1917
French Artist and Sculptor

What Career?

Charlotte Backman

1

I only remember one thing about career planning in high school. Our teacher asked us to research all aspects of a career we might like to pursue – such as the required education, potential employers, and average salaries. I picked massage therapy. I may as well have picked race car driver because no one took my choice seriously. In fact, nobody discussed my choice at all – they ignored it, or as I imagined the adults saying, "gently steered me in a different direction."

Back in 1973 people still lumped massage therapy in with "adult entertainment" in the phone book and considered it much too risqué a profession for a wholesome middle class girl from the suburbs of Orange County.

So, having no idea what I wanted to do, other than learn more stuff about people and life, I applied to college like the rest of my friends and headed off to UCLA to get myself an English degree. My college experience exposed me to a much bigger world than my sequestered life in Tustin had allowed. I learned to think about big issues in a different way, changed my religion, changed my politics, and changed my beliefs about what I could do and who I was. At graduation, however, I still had no idea what career would satisfy me for the rest of my working days. Most of my friends in the liberal arts crowd didn't know either. Those serious science and pre-med students, who knew the career they wanted to pursue, were far away on the other side of campus.

I don't remember how I got my first job in the real world – doing copywriting and paste-up for a small real estate firm run by an arrogant, insensitive jerk. After I worked for four months at minimum wage, the jerk laid me off two weeks before Christmas, along with the rest of his meager staff. He told us he would hire us back after the holidays. That way he wouldn't have to pay us vacation days. He complained mightily when I filed for unemployment insurance because employers have to pay a percentage. What an arrogant, insensitive, *cheap* jerk. I never went back.

However, it did lead to a job in advertising, a definite step up the career ladder. At the tiny agency, everyone's job title had slashes: President/Creative Director/Account Executive, Vice President/Account Executive/Bookkeeper/Media Buyer, and me, Everything Else plus some of theirs too. We all got along well, I learned about the advertising business, and felt like a responsible adult for the first time. After three years the agency grew, hired a new president, and I was out, just in time to sign up for a job under my favorite boss, my Dad.

Dad was a contractor in Orange County. He had a small regular crew and had just gotten a job remodeling a beautiful home on the water in Newport Beach. Since the project would take many months to complete, I signed up, strapping on my tool belt every morning and learning as I went. I'm good with my hands – that's why I wanted to be a massage therapist – and I highly recommend demolishing a kitchen as one of the great stress relievers of all time. Mostly I did menial work, cleaned up after the guys, and appreciated the time I spent with my dad.

It would seem like getting a job on a construction crew would be a detour from my advertising career path, but that would assume I'd *decided* on a career path. In truth I still had no idea where I was going. In the meantime, I got married and moved back to Orange County, where a young couple could still buy a home.

This led directly to my next job: Order Administrator in a Hewlett-Packard sales office. When my husband and I settled into our new house (actually a 1925 fixer-upper), I drew a circle around the house on the map with a compass. I had had enough of freeways in Los Angeles, and I refused to commute long distance if I could avoid it. It was icing on the cake that HP was considered one of the best companies to work for; *I* liked it because it was 10 minutes from my house. Now *there's* a smart way to choose a job, huh? Lucky for me, it worked out, and I spent the next nine years there, learning and moving up through various administrative jobs. However, when the company downsized and offered me a severance package, it should be no surprise that I took it and moved on.

I suppose I could have gritted my teeth, looked ahead to a cozy retirement package, and stayed in the corporate world. However, three years before I left HP, life sent me a wake-up call. My husband's mother was diagnosed with a brain tumor and six months later she died. She had been healthy and happy and then she was gone. I realized that nothing prevented that from happening to me too. I thought, "Am I really happy? What would I regret not doing if I died tomorrow? Massage therapy, here I come."

By the 1980s, massage therapy had become a respectable job with plenty of training programs in traditional and holistic methods. I started a part-time practice after work and on weekends, carting my massage table to people's homes and offices and soothing their tired, stressed muscles. I got referrals from a chiropractor, didn't have to advertise, and had very little overhead. And most important, I was finally doing something useful and meaningful. I made my clients feel better. "Maybe I'm meant to be in the healing professions," I thought.

Many of my clients experienced emotional as well as physical release when I massaged them. Since I'd always been interested in psychology, I decided that I could facilitate healing on more than a physical level and enrolled in a two-year certification course in body-mind psychotherapy. As life would have it, I graduated from that course the same month I left HP. All at once it felt like I had an open road ahead of me. I was 38 years old, childless, separated from my husband, and free to recreate my life.

The next month my Dad fell and broke a hip, had prostate surgery, and spent the next two years in and out of nursing homes and hospitals. My mother and I took turns visiting him regularly. After he died, my grandmother went into a nursing home and Mom and I did the same for her. Perhaps all that caretaking, although done willingly, made me think again about whether I wanted a life devoted to healing. Although I had only a part-time massage practice, I was burned out. I stopped massaging, got a part-time job in a property management office, treaded water, and waited for inspiration.

I belong to a group that meets every Wednesday morning at UC Irvine called the Inside Edge. About 100 people gather to eat breakfast and listen to speakers on topics such as psychology, spirituality, business and culture. One day the topic was Art as a Spiritual Practice. The speaker was a local Laguna Beach artist who specialized in painting mandalas, a type of spiritual art from India. I signed up right away for the speaker's next workshop, making mandalas on black paper with colored pencils.

I loved it. A whole wonderful world opened up before me. However, since I'd received a C in art in high school, I was skittish and shy about making art. I spent the next year playing with acrylic paints, doing whatever I felt like and not showing it to anyone but my husband and a handful of people I trusted. I wanted to find my own way, with no one to influence the process with praise or criticism. Finally I felt ready to take another class, this time a week of painting at a retreat in Northern California. The mandala I painted there was the first of more than 200, and the surprising beginning of a new career in making and teaching art. Wait, what am I saying? If a career is something you expect to do for the rest of your working life, then it's my *first* career, and it didn't begin until I was 40.

If I were to mentor someone just graduating or *anyone* who didn't have a clue about what would sustain their whole physical/emotional/spiritual being throughout their life, first I'd ask some questions.

--What have you always liked to do, no matter what anyone else thinks of the process or the product?

--What motivates you to get up in the morning or keeps you up late at night because you are so excited about doing it?

Second, I'd say do it, and do whatever else you have to do to *keep* doing it, as long as it is deeply sustaining. Whether or not it can or will become a career is beside the point. Wait tables while you write your novel. Practice law while you study to be an herbalist. If something doesn't feel quite right, keep exploring and experimenting. Don't get hung up about what your friends or relatives or your own inner critic say you should or shouldn't do. Whose life is it? (OK, if your burning desire is to, say, rob banks, listen to your mother on that one and pick something else.) Keep curious and let life reveal its wonders to you. They will unfold like flowers if you are patient and persistent.

Sometimes life feels all wrong and you tell yourself you're a loser or a no-talent mess who is going nowhere and destined to be miserable the rest of your life. Maybe you will, but chances are very good you won't. Here's the bottom line: life will *not* turn out like you planned. If you don't know where you're going, you're still guaranteed to get *somewhere*, and it may not be that bad a place to end up! Trust the journey and make it a good journey.

"It's been very important throughout my career that I've met all the guys I've copied, because at each stage they've said, 'Don't play like me, play like you.' "

Eric Clapton
1945-
British Musician and Singer

If I'm so Smart, Why Is My Career Such a Mess?

John Hall

2

S lam-bam—the question, "If I'm So Smart, Why Is My Career Such a Mess?" struck my brain like a bolt of lighting as I drove home from a decade long job as the manager of a clinical laboratory in Newport Beach, California. In some ways the question didn't make sense. After all I had achieved much of the American Dream: nice home, money in the bank, investments that were going well, and a loving, supportive wife. However, it became all too clear after that question "infected" my brain that my career was a mess because it was founded on a series of potluck decisions based on opportunities of the moment.

Quiet Desperation

I did not have a career; I had a series of jobs, and to paraphrase Henry David Thoreau, I led "a life of quiet desperation." It wasn't that I couldn't handle the work, either intellectually or physically, or wasn't making enough money. The work held no joy or personal satisfaction for me. The thought of spending another 30 years doing the same work was mind numbing.

11

Reflecting back on that long ago drive home, I realized that I had spent more time planning vacations and my social life than my career. If only I had known at 18 what I knew at 35. However, life doesn't work that way. More often than not we make our most important decision, the selection of what may well become our life's work, as a pimply faced adolescent, without the life experience, knowledge or guidance to make an informed choice.

You Have To Major In Something.

The majority of men and women, from PhDs to dropouts, drift along, ending up where the stream of their lives takes them, taking the course of least resistance in their careers. I was no exception. When I graduated from high school, I enrolled at Ohio State University in Columbus, Ohio. I had no idea what I wanted to do with my life so had no idea what to major in. As a result I took all the required courses, like math, English, social studies, physical education, ROTC, history and a bunch of electives. I also dabbled at three majors, Geology, Secondary Education, and Biology. After about two and a half years a counselor called me into his office and said, "Kid, if you ever expect to graduate, you are going to have to major in something." So, after an in-depth, twelve-minute review of my transcript, the counselor said, "It looks to me like biology with a minor in history is your best option."

"Great," I said, and off I went to get a degree majoring in biology with a minor in history.

No problem, I'm smart—and I Have a Profession!

A semester before completing my degree, a buddy told me that the College of Medicine was looking for biology majors for a one-year training program in a new, specialized area of medical technology, cytology. Neither one of us knew what cytology was, but if they accepted us, they would pay us well during the training and guarantee us a job when we completed the course. It was not yet an accredited degree program but we were assured that it soon would be accredited. Thirty biology majors applied, twelve were accepted, and ten of us graduated from the training. I then did almost two years of cancer research at Ohio State University's pediatric hospital.

Cytology, this new area of medical technology, was accredited for both bachelors and masters degrees at Ohio State University several years after I moved to southern California. I did not want to go back to Ohio State for the three to six months needed to finish the newly accredited degrees. Technically I was a well-educated degreeless nincompoop. No big deal. I was young and smart — I'd take care of that little problem — someday.

My first job in research wasn't my idea of a long-term career. However, it fell into my lap and I was young and had plenty of time to figure out how to get on the right track. "No big deal," I thought. "I am smart. I'll know when the right opportunity comes along." In less than a year I had a nice apartment, a sports car, and a great social life with lots of pretty young ladies to date. The job wasn't what I wanted to do for the rest of my life, but I knew something would come along. I was smart and had a professional education.

Hey, it's a No Brainer.

One day I received a phone call from a college buddy, a technician in a hospital laboratory in Peoria, Illinois. He said they needed a cytology technician and it paid a lot more money than I was currently making — so I was off to Peoria. No career planning, no thinking about how this job might impact my career long term. Six months later, someone I met at a professional meeting offered me a position in a private lab in Newport Beach, California. Wow, California — sun, the beach, beautiful girls in bikinis, and the job paid even more! This was a no brainer — so it was "California, here I come!"

Quiet Desperation

Several years after arriving in California, I met and married Nancy, a bright, understanding, lovely schoolteacher from Pittsburgh, Pennsylvania. Soon we had a nice home, a mortgage, nice vacations, car payments and all the stuff that should have made me happy. But, over the next few years I developed a feeling of quiet desperation about my career. As I reflected on my early working years, I realized that I felt trapped by the Golden Handcuffs of a comfortable middle class life. But hey, I was still relatively young, smart and had a profession. Then, on that fateful drive home, "slam-bam," I came face to face with reality. If I'm So Smart, Why Is My Career Such a Mess?

Starting Over In Midlife

In my quiet desperation, I sought the help of a career counselor. I learned that I am drawn to the helping professions, psychology, teaching, speaking, and writing. Hey, wait a minute—this should have been obvious: I had been a Division Governor in Toastmasters, in charge of 30 clubs, and won a number of speaking awards; I was President of the Los Angeles Area Chapter of the National Speakers Association; I had read numerous books on psychology and for years subscribed to the magazine *Psychology Today* and read every issue from cover to cover. Why did it take a career counselor to make a connection between these obvious interests and a career? Perhaps I did not trust my own judgment and did not understand how I might make a decent income with what I viewed as hobbies.

Under the guidance of my career counselor I completed 11 information interviews with successful men and women in psychology, teaching, training and development, and outplacement. Putting all the information together, I decided to become an outplacement counselor. Outplacement involved psychology, speaking, and training and it fit my need to be in a helping profession. After making the decision to go into outplacement counseling, I developed a five-year career plan, which included a mission statement and milestones, with the ultimate goal of going into business for myself. Following my five-year plan, I completed an undergraduate degree in six months then went on to complete graduate degrees in psychology and career counseling. I then joined a large national career management firm, then a regional outplacement firm and finally went into private practice.

There is one more critical element in my successful midlife career change, my wife Nancy. Without her love, support, and encouragement my transition would have been much, much more difficult.

When I tell my story to audiences large and small, whether at professional associations, church groups, or universities, I always ask, by a show of hands, how many can relate? How many have felt that sense of quiet desperation about their careers? Consistently 80% of the men and women in those audiences indicate that they have experienced their own sense of career dissatisfaction, bewilderment and quiet desperation.

Question

Are you one of the 20 percent who truly enjoy you career? Or are you drifting wherever the stream of life takes you?

"I've missed more than 9,000 shots in my career. I've lost almost 300 games. 26 times I've been trusted to take the game winning shot and missed. I've failed over and over and over again in my life. And that is why I succeed."

Michael Jordan
1963-
Professional Basketball Player and Businessman

Changing My Mind

3

Steve Amos

So how did a quiet, shy kid grow up to be a leader? How did a kid who flunked spelling write books? When does an engineer become a speaker? How did a boy from a dysfunctional family find peace? How did he grow up to be a confident, competent man?

When I look back, the big changes in my life occurred when I changed my mind. The changes did not happen in an instant and often took years. Often I never initially noticed the change in myself. However, every time I changed my thinking, I changed what I thought about, what I did, what I did not do, how I reacted, and how I lived.

One of the first changes in my thinking happened at the beginning of eighth grade. I had shot up three inches over the summer. Boys being boys, some bigger guys in my class picked on me. The truly strong, athletic ones never picked on me. My trouble came from the ones just a little bigger than me who wanted to make up for their insecurity.

One morning, the first after summer vacation, I walked up to a group of boys. Someone announced my arrival. One of the smaller boys in my class said, "Let's pick on him." He turned and looked down to where I used to be standing. Then he looked up to where I was now towering over him. He turned back to the group and listened sheepishly to the laughter of the other boys and me. I had learned bullies wanted someone easy to pick on and made up my mind to stand up to bullies no matter how big they were. Bullies quickly learned to leave me alone.

College

I was a smart and very lazy student at school. I read the homework because I liked to. I answered test questions because I had to. But study? I studied for three tests in my last three years of high school. My grades floundered all year until the last marking period when I worked to get an A+ every time and at least an A on the final. I was a terrible student. However, reading the textbook and doing the homework was enough to breeze through high school.

I started college with horrible study habits. I knew doing well required me to memorize large amounts of material and I was terrible at it. I'm lucky to remember my name.

I went to college to be an engineer. I had no idea what kind of engineer and had no clue what real world companies wanted.

Engineering was a tough discipline. In four years I took only six non-engineering classes. I struggled just to pass. In my junior year, I failed both semesters and ended up with a 1.5 grade point average. I even messed up three courses trying to pass one particularly difficult instructor's course. It was definitely not a dean's list performance.

For three summers I had a good job at Eastman Kodak, where I replaced factory workers on vacation. If I had quit college and stayed, I would have earned about the same or more with overtime than as an engineer. However, it was repetitive, physical work. That summer I was depressed. My girlfriend had dumped me during the second semester. I worked, licked my wounds and missed my ex-girlfriend. Then I got mad - first at the world, then at myself, and finally at those who doubted me. I decided I wouldn't quit school and vowed to finish college no matter how long it took.

I brought that decision and attitude back to school that fall. I took additional classes, studied long hours, worked hard, budgeted time, cut down my social life, interviewed for jobs, got hired, and got one more B than I needed to graduate. I did what I vowed to do because I chose to finish my education no matter what.

Entering the World of Work

When my first semester grades arrived with As and Bs, my goal of graduating seemed within reach so I started looking for a job for after graduation. A friend gave me a great idea: schedule some interviews with companies I wasn't serious about to get practice. So I wasn't nervous or scared about interviewing with this company from Connecticut. Heck, I didn't even know where Connecticut was. Since I was presentable, polite, and able to answer basic questions, I got invited to visit the plant. I had my first interview and then rolled confidently through a series of interviews without a clue as to what I was doing.

After three other interviews with different companies, I received two job offers for better money than I expected. I needed to choose. One position was as a plant engineer for a Chlorine Caustic company close to my college. The other was from my practice interview. The plant engineer paid a bit more but Connecticut had lower taxes. The decision hinged on a question I asked employees at each company about their career history and age. The people in New York looked five years older than their age. The people in Connecticut were five years older than they looked. I wanted to live a long life and chose the better life over the higher salary.

Although I was proud of graduating despite my troubles, I felt bad about graduating in the lower third of my class. I knew I could have done better. Several years later a friend asked how many students were in my class. I said there were 662 students my first semester but only 220 graduated. A lot changed majors but more quit or flunked out. I am now proud of finishing in the lower third of the one third that graduated. That different perspective changed my outlook. When situations come up, I look for other ways to judge them.

I was very shy until my mid twenties. At that point I realized I was doing as well as most people. I had a good job, paid my bills, had good friends, and contributed to society. Everyone else had times when they were lost, confused, and struggled. It is honorable to muddle through life and I was doing as well or better than most people. So I gave up thinking shy (except occasionally) and took pride in my accomplishments.

Great companies do fail. My first company, Pratt & Whitney Aircraft, had great products but had stopped delivering on time. They learned a powerful lesson. Customers will go elsewhere! My second defense company, United Nuclear, only had one customer. When the US government decided it only needed one supplier of Navy nuclear plants after I had been there four years, UNC laid off almost everyone in my division. That started one of the hardest and best times of my life.

Unemployed and Better

I tell people that being unemployed for six months was one of the best experiences of my life. They think I am crazy. Then I would tell you that thought was crazy. At the time I was stressed out. I had bought my first home nine months before and was draining my savings while I looked for a job. I had always found work easily. In fact work often found me. For the first time I had to hunt for a job and I was not good at it. Fortunately Joe Koneski, an experienced headhunter, helped me write my resume and taught me how to present my abilities in an interview.

I did other things to counter the stress. I purchased my first answering machine so I could leave home without fear of missing a call, exercised frequently and walked with a firm stride with my head held high. I greeted people with a loud hello, not my shy voice, as practice for interviews to come. Of course I was still nervous and worried. However, I took this advice, straight from *What Color is Your Parachute*, and it worked. When I interviewed I looked relaxed, confident and energetic. If only I felt relaxed and confident.

As my attitude improved, interviewing became easier. I knew I was good at my work and knew I came across as a genuine person. Once I was forced to think about them, I was surprised at how many successful projects I had forgotten. Instead of being afraid when I went on an interview, I began to look forward to finding out about the new company, the employees, and finding ways to contribute to their success.

Becoming an Expert

I changed my mind again when I took a course with Barbara Winter on "How to be an Expert." Barbara has taught thousands how to be self employed and how to focus on their gifts, which we do easily and effortlessly and which we often take for granted. After much reflection, I realized that my core skill is problem solving. I have always loved to find root causes and offer solutions. Barbara's course also taught me how important it is to market my gifts.

I set a new mission at work: Our purpose is to protect the property of our customers. I researched our products and our competitor's products. I became an expert on lock cylinders of all kinds, their usages, strengths, and weaknesses. I studied crime trends to find new product ideas. This extra effort paid off. When marketing wanted new ways to sell products, I provided the business reason and root problem for them to use. I helped develop five new products and tools to solve these problems. We redesigned production so we could build to order faster. My value rose because I thought differently about business.

The business market share grew from third place to a very competitive second by consistent on time delivery, good quality, fair prices, and creating new products that met the customer's needs. We no longer needed to carry large inventories because we shipped orders in five business days versus two months for our competitors. We became a good investment. After my company was bought for the fourth time in seven years and the business cycle slowed, I sent a couple of headhunters a resume just in case. That's how I wound up in Texas and California. A recruiter called to see if I would work in Texas. They would relocate me, pay for selling my house, pay living expenses until the house sold, help with financing, and pay a bonus. It was worth a look.

Moving Cross Country

Life is quite different in the "land of steady habits" (Connecticut) versus "where everything is bigger" (Texas). In Connecticut I wore a tie even when working on greasy machines. In Texas no one wore a tie after their interview and they were proud of it. Cowboy boots are considered proper dress for jeans, business suits and everything in between. So on the first day I wore my boots. The new guy sounded funny with a Connecticut/New York accent, but he looked like one of them. My major adjustment was to slow down my speech so I could be understood. After six months the local drawl started to appear, y'all understand?

Usually a new employee learns about the company first: who knows whom, how they go about making decisions and other protocols. My first week in Texas, at the first interplant meeting with who knew whom on the conference call, we discussed a new product line launch that was failing with a 50% yield, horrible for production. The design engineer and product manager had no clue as to exactly what was wrong. I listened and waited. There were not enough parts to replace the scrap these people were making. If they kept going it would become a bigger crisis. After 40 minutes, I interrupted. "Let me get this straight, we have a 50% yield on the start up line?" It was confirmed. "Don't you think it is time to shut down production? We can't make replacement parts fast enough to replace the losses."

Production people hate to stop production. They will do extensive workarounds, jump through impossible hoops, but they hate stopping a line. All that labor standing around. What are we getting paid for? So after a pregnant pause at all three plants, I repeated, "It is time to stop production. It is costing too much money to run the line until you figure out what is wrong." The result of this discussion was that the people who had not met me wanted to, and my new plant respected me for standing up.

It was a very productive time. I expedited design reviews, problem solved new products, helped install ISO 9000, and trained engineers. Productivity increased 10.2% and the plant became the preferred supplier for Black & Decker locks. A promotion soon followed at the main Southern California office.

Changes Happen with a New Boss

Life changed again with a new boss. I understood the urgency of developing new products but not the chaos he deliberately created. Eventually an engineer I truly respected replaced me. Heck I would have hired him ahead of me. I became a man without a real position, got poor reviews, was frustrated, became depressed, and eventually had to leave the job I had thought of as home. It was terrible since I did not have another plan. Later I realized the problem was not that I had turned into a terrible worker but the new manager wanted my salary for another position. That knowledge alone stopped the depression.

Once again my weaknesses were exposed. A workaholic without a job is sad. My social life was okay, but I had no significant other to support, encourage, and kick my butt. It was time to change again.

I joined a religious group of positive thinking business people. I was a classic "Lilac and Poinsettia Catholic" who would attend church only during the holidays. This group focused on fixing us up before showing us the good word. The most important lesson I learned was we are here to help others. Serve others first, and success will follow. It was not a quick transition, nor an easy one to change my thinking. It is very hard to let old habits go. But if you persist, fail a few times, and start to do some good you will learn.

I became an entrepreneur with their support. The first business failed, and while looking for a job I met my wife. I worked for another entrepreneur. He was a friend of my cousin and knew I was looking for work. I went to work part time, which led to 50 to 60 hour workweeks, and three years of work. When he took a sabbatical, I began to consult.

After six years of being a member, I became the leader of the career group. Here I worked with mentors, watched experts volunteer their gifts and occasionally gave prepared presentations. When a scheduled speaker did not show for one meeting, I taught a lesson on his subject on the spot.

I enjoy helping others. My skills, problem solving, and experience in a diversity of industries is a resource. I also listen to the advice of the people I hang out with and help my mentors. My goal is to mentor other people like they did me.

Who Do You Want to Be?

Now, how do you become the person you want to be? The simple answer is to find examples of who you want to become. Act as if you are already what you want to be. Repeat until you learn how. You will be comfortable and do what you dream of. Just get started.

A Perfect Match

Janet L. Newcomb

4

How did an employee of a very large corporation become an entrepreneur? It may surprise you to know that a Fortune 500 company was the best school I could have attended to learn what I needed to know to be an effective coach, consultant and small business owner. In the beginning, I wasn't thinking about a career. I just needed to get a job until I figured out what to do next. What I learned about careers over the next 30+ years can be summed up in three basic principles:

1. Know and honor who you are.
2. Understand the current needs in the marketplace.
3. Look for the best match you can make between 1 and 2.

What were the most significant experiences that shaped my career at this "corporate university?"

We all start somewhere – just start!

When I started working, there weren't a lot of career choices for women. You could get married, go to school until you found someone to marry, or work as a teacher, nurse, or secretary until you married. I got a job as a secretary at Douglas Aircraft Company. I worked for many interesting people over the next eight years – engineers, Ph.D. scientists doing aerospace analysis, customer financing experts, and marketing managers for Army, Navy, and Air Force programs. The pay and benefits were good and I earned regular promotions as I climbed from my entry level position toward the top of the secretarial career ladder. Once you get in the door, it's definitely easier to see opportunities that exist.

Be willing to try new things.

My first husband was offered a job at American University in Washington, D.C., so this California girl moved 2,684 miles across the country to a city where I didn't know anyone. This adventure definitely expanded my horizons. By then, Douglas had merged and become McDonnell Douglas. Luckily, I was able to transfer to their Washington sales office and continue accruing retirement benefits. I was surprised how much this big risk added to my life. I enjoyed the East Coast and found our nation's capitol an exciting place to live and work. The four seasons, the architecture and the sophisticated social/cultural experiences were spectacular. Since one of my husband's students was married to a woman who worked at the White House, we were invited to many special events – diplomatic receptions, the Presidential Inauguration, Christmas Eve services at The National Cathedral, even the White House Easter egg roll. I still remember standing on the White House lawn when Nixon's helicopter lifted off to start his ground-breaking trip to China. Heady stuff for a young couple in their 20s! These experiences are responsible for my lifelong interest in leadership and ethical governance.

Interest and Instinct

My marriage failed and I moved back to California, going to work for the Vice President of Government Marketing in Long Beach. I soon realized that, unless the President's secretary died, there was nowhere else to advance on the secretarial career ladder. So, I went back to school at night and finally graduated from CSU Long Beach. How did I pick my Sociology major? It was purely interest and instinct. I looked at the catalogue and decided which major had the most classes that appealed to me. I didn't have anything definite in mind other than getting my Bachelor's degree but this experience ignited a lifelong interest in learning.

Everyone needs support while learning and growing.

My boss, a wonderful mentor, believed in me and knew I wouldn't be satisfied to be a secretary forever. When I completed my degree, he helped me transfer to the Contracts Department where I started out at the very bottom of a new career ladder – handling government property management and contract terminations. It was boring at first but it allowed me to get my foot in another door and begin to grow in a whole new direction. Eventually I became a Senior Contract Administrator, negotiating multi-million dollar contracts with the Air Force and Navy. I learned to lead and participate in a team, analyze government RFP's, prepare responsive proposals and negotiate contract prices, terms and conditions. Communicating effectively, something I particularly enjoy, was a big part of working with team members, government representatives, and our subcontractors. An unexpected benefit was "seeing the USA" all expenses paid. I had opportunities to travel to many cities I had never visited – New Orleans, Philadelphia, Norfolk, San Antonio, and Dallas – in addition to returning many times to my old hometown, Washington, D.C. I was fortunate to work for and with many men who mentored me and gave me increased responsibilities as I demonstrated my ability and interest.

Blind Luck, Creativity and Persistence

One day a co-worker's wife encouraged me to apply for a scholarship to law school. I have always been a bit of a "crusader rabbit" with a strong interest in social justice, so I thought, "Why not?" All I had to do was write an essay and submit my resume. I never thought I would win and had pretty much forgotten about it when one day I received a call telling me I had won one of ten nationwide scholarships to Western State University in Fullerton. Wow! I was going to law school! At this point in my life I was remarried, had a two-year-old son and three teenage stepchildren. What was I thinking? It never occurred to me that this was a little crazy. (Sometimes it's a good thing when you don't realize that something might not be possible.) For four years I went to school part time, worked nearly full time, helped raise four children and still traveled on my job. I convinced the Director of the Contracts Department (also a Western State grad) to charge me with one day of vacation every week, divided between Tuesday and Thursday afternoons. This allowed me to attend two afternoon classes and one night class and finish all my credits in four years. When I ran out of vacation, I asked him to pay me 32 hours each week instead of 40 so that I could maintain the same schedule. Fortunately, I worked for people who not only supported me and my career but were very flexible (unusual in large corporations). I even had a chance to study international law at Cambridge University in England one summer by using a combination of accrued vacation and unpaid leave. I'm not sure how I did it except to say, "Where there's a will, there's a way." I loved the intellectual challenge of law school and thought obtaining a law degree would enhance my status and pay. That turned out to be true - but not in a way I could have predicted.

A Perfect Match

In my last semester of law school, MDC posted an ad for an ombudsman. The job was a combination of mediator, organizational troubleshooter, corporate critic and change agent, reporting to the president of the aircraft division with

52,000 employees. I thought, "That's a job I'd do for free if I could afford it." It sounded fascinating. However, I was in the middle of another divorce, studying for finals and getting ready for the bar exam. It didn't seem like good timing. I didn't apply right away but I couldn't get the job out of my mind and I couldn't resist the intuitive sense that this was a once-in-a-lifetime opportunity. On the very last day, I turned in my application. Over 100 people went through a nearly six-month selection process. I got the job! There were two of us in the office – a man who had been vice president of engineering, taking his last assignment prior to retirement, and me. Equal opportunity had come to the aerospace industry. What is it they say? Timing is everything. I held this job for nine years and it was a perfect match for my extroverted and creative personality. The analytical skills honed in law school served me well in diagnosing cases likely to result in litigation if they weren't resolved. I loved helping people and I thrived on the continual challenge of new problems to solve. That law degree paid off when I negotiated a 30% pay increase with my promotion.

Network, Network, Network
One of the highlights of the ombudsman position came when I represented MDC on a People-to-People Mediation Delegation to the People's Republic of China. I never imagined my ombudsman role would involve climbing on the Great Wall of China, traveling with the first woman judge in England, or eating deep fried scorpions! I also spent six years on the board of directors of the Corporate Ombudsman Association and participated as a faculty member in the creation and delivery of their national training programs. As I served on a number of community non-profit boards and spoke about effective conflict resolution skills I expanded my professional network. Activities outside the company always paid off for me. Often I made important connections that led

to other connections and opportunities. At other times I practiced and developed new skills without worrying about whether I was qualified to do them or not. I even met my current business partner at an International Coach Federation dinner long before I became a member. What are the odds that I would sit down at the same table next to another entrepreneur with similar interests and values who also wasn't a member of ICF and begin a relationship that would develop into a California "C" corporation? You never know where your networking will take you and it helps not to be totally dependent on your employer. We all know that these days circumstances can change in a heartbeat.

Disappointing events can propel you to better things.
Eventually the company split into two separate parts, military and commercial, and went through numerous reorganizations and downsizings. The ombudsman office was closed prior to a second merger, with the Boeing Company. I had assumed the ombudsman job would be my last assignment prior to retirement, but I wasn't old enough to retire! I also had too many years invested to leave, a classic case of golden handcuffs.

I transferred to Human Resources, where I had a number of employee/organizational development responsibilities such as surveys, executive education, career counseling, performance development strategies, exit interviews/trend analyses, mentoring, management consulting, diversity education, and assessments. I started a Master's Degree in Organizational Management through the University of Phoenix online program but dropped out about halfway through when my mother was dying. I also trained as an Executive Coach through a program Boeing subcontracted to the Center for Creative Leadership. I ended my corporate career managing the Career Transition Center that provided outplacement services for over 5,000 employees as Boeing began to shut down the commercial division of McDonnell Douglas.

Seeing the Opportunity in Change

What now? This was a *major* career and life transition. I was definitely seasoned. I already had some coach training. My very broad business background and natural thinking style made it easy to relate to executives. The executive coaching field was growing and seemed like a natural fit so I signed up for a formal eight-month personal/organizational coach training program at The Hudson Institute of Santa Barbara. I didn't just learn about coaching. I also learned the concept of "portfolio career" - a little bit of a lot of different things. Perfect for me! I'm writing, traveling, and building several businesses with a partner who is nearly 20 years younger than I am. In addition to traditional executive coaching, I do leadership development work and assist many types of professionals with career transitions.

Conclusions

When I look back, I see that I never had a concrete career plan. However, my career did have a synchronistic (although largely unpredictable) progression. I have reinvented myself a number of times, sometimes because I wanted to and sometimes because I had to. My current work is far more entrepreneurial, although I couldn't be doing it nearly as well without my prior business experience. I have worked in every business function except manufacturing and learned what works (and doesn't) to create and maintain a sustainable business. I recognize now that I was an intrapreneur[1] all those years.

---

[1] Intrapreneur = one who acts in an entrepreneurial fashion inside a large organization.

If there are "secrets" to share, what would they be? Here are my tips:

- Follow your interests and instincts.
- Honor your natural talents.
- Stay alert and open to opportunities as they present themselves.
- Don't compromise your values.
- Leverage relationships with people you admire and who believe in you.
- Stay actively engaged with your community, build your network, and never have all your eggs in one basket.
- Choose to see change as an opportunity rather than a threat.

Regrets? Only that aerospace was very traditional and male-dominated. As a woman, I probably had to work harder to get ahead. However, I was part of the generation that fought for women's equality in the workplace so it might not have been easy anywhere. I've met some amazing people and had some very interesting experiences. I'm still enjoying my work and can't imagine ever completely retiring. All in all, it's been a great ride. I look forward to what might happen next. I hope you always will too.

Creating Opportunities
In the Current Economy

Jacqueline A. Soares

5

Even at the ripe old age of three, I was delegating to my younger sister the job of smashing avocados against the house and leading her down busy streets to see the cow on top of the market. I wanted deeply to know and experience my surroundings and was secure in my own decisions.

By my adolescent years I was definitely developing into an "entrepreneur in the making." Life gave me many opportunities to demonstrate my natural tendencies and learn important lessons:

- Selling my Easter basket to a neighbor for a quarter (raising venture capital)
- Play acting with neighborhood children and participating in school talent shows (communication and presentation skills)
- Kool-aid stand (cash flow may not be sufficient for hours invested)
- Girl Scouts (sales and tasty fringe benefits, handling money, working with a team, leadership)
- Junior Achievement, where I bartered my sewing talents for others' services (negotiation skills)

- Restaurant hostess (various people skills)
- Manager of bowling alley food court (the importance of presence – I was only 17; they thought I was 21)
- Assembling wetsuits - I liked the work and worked hard but got fired for leaving late for lunch (understanding different personalities - following the rules is more important to some people than getting the job done)

By 1984, I had a husband, four children, three dogs and a cat and needed to find a way to contribute to the family income while still being a wife and mom. Once again I tapped into my creative and entrepreneurial inclinations and found opportunities that taught me a lot about business and provided the flexibility I needed:

- Buying and selling antiques, glassware and jewelry: I loved the hunt for a great bargain and a good profit margin. Probably the most important thing I learned is that I prefer the educational/consultative approach to hard-core sales.
- Shady Lady, custom Victorian lampshades: I identified a need (trend) and created a niche. Learned about purchasing in bulk, pre-planning the needs of my clientele, keeping up with trends in the industry and the importance of good customer service. I learned about marketing the product and meeting the customer's needs while working with several boutique antique stores and some major interior designers. I also found that custom designs and quality couldn't be easily replicated. Lack of capital and emotional support prevented growth of the business. I did learn how important it is to team up with the right people (personally and professionally). I also noticed that I was happiest and peacefully centered when I was sewing and creating something.

In 1990, my divorce precipitated a major life transition. Thinking that a more stable corporate job, along with a more predictable structure, would be *the answer*, I went to work for the leasing department of a large copier company. It was a temp job to start with, subbing in for the office manager who was on leave. I knew nothing about the leasing business or working with corporate rules and regulations, but I'm a quick learner.

When the office manager decided not to return, I was offered her job. I worked effectively with the sales manager, vice-president of finance, and the company president. However, after three years I noticed that there were no advancement opportunities. I didn't have a college education and the only female executive in the company headed the Human Resource department. The rest of the executives were men and this wasn't going to change any time soon. My salary wasn't enough to support the growing needs of four children so I began to consider going back to school. Perhaps education was *the answer*.

I continued to work at my corporate job until one day I became very sick. After being off work for a week and doing some serious reflecting, I realized I needed to go to school full time to make my new plan work. I did my research and found that by applying for state aid I could raise enough money to go to school full time. Along with scholarships, Pell grants and other money available for re-entering students (nice way to say "older") I could actually end up with more money, have medical benefits for me and my children, and obtain a higher education that would help me find a better position. I resigned from my job as this solution also let me be around the children more – a need that became painfully obvious as they entered their adolescent years. (There should be a law against anyone having more than two teenagers in a household!) While this plan was a good long-term solution, the arrangement wasn't without its short-term problems. We had to give up our condo and move into a motel to qualify for housing assistance and it was nearly a year before we found an apartment we could manage based on our new income status.

I started classes at Coastline College and picked up house cleaning work between my schedule and the children's. There were a lot of displaced employees returning to college in the late 90's so at least I wasn't the oldest adult in class. I also found out why academics had always been such a struggle for me – I'm dyslexic – reading and writing don't come easily. I had to work twice as hard as some. Fortunately, I listen well and comprehend what I hear, along with being able to make good verbal presentations. I also met people along the way who helped me learn study and research skills that worked for me. I've also learned to get help for when I have to write something. (Everyone has strengths and weaknesses.)

The housecleaning business grew and I continued to go to school full time. Housecleaning was hands on, physical and fast-paced, with low overhead and high return. It was customer service oriented and very satisfying to make a difference in someone's home and life. It also provided a very flexible schedule. I graduated with my AA and legal assistant certificate and was accepted into the CSU Long Beach sociology program in 1997.

While at CSULB I was able to barter my paralegal skills for mediation training. Then I brokered a deal between the university and The Mediation Center which allowed me to satisfy a required internship in sociology and acquire paralegal experience working in their family law department. I managed client cases, developed program material, trained and supervised volunteers, prepared legal documents, and participated in mediation sessions. In addition to acquiring family mediation certificates and experience, I was paid well.

I walked across the graduation stage in 2000, the same year my father died. Things were changing fast because of shifts in the local and global economies. Large corporations were beginning to move work out of state or into foreign lands. Many smaller companies were starting up, creating different types of employers and benefit packages (and lack of benefits). I quickly saw how my education and experience could be blended to open my own business with a partner I had met at the Mediation Center. Alternative to Litigation was a legal document preparation and mediation service. Partnerships are funny things. My partner was a great person, just not well suited for the high-risk atmosphere of a start up. Thankfully, we are still friends. I learned that if we don't pay attention to what each person brings to the table to support the continued growth of a partnership, it will die – much like a living, breathing organism that is not fed the right nutrients.

On my own again, I founded Alternative Resolutions, another legal document preparation and mediation service. Entrepreneurs have a tendency to do the work themselves first and then take time looking for or training new people, so as a sole proprietor there were long hours but lots of flexibility. I also concurrently worked part-time for an attorney, managing her legal office – billing, document preparation, and client interface. Along the way, I also volunteered on a number of boards, usually to enhance my exposure to a field I was working in. It's a great way to keep current, develop networking opportunities and develop or practice new skills.

What are the most important things I have learned overall, especially about myself? I see these lessons clustering into three broad categories:

- **Family** – Family life has taught me selflessness – sometimes too much. These experiences have forced me to look at my own self care and balance helping others while fine-tuning the physical-emotional-spiritual aspects of my own life. After all, what am I really teaching my children if I always settle for the burnt toast in life? Being selfless eventually becomes unmanageable when taken to the extreme.

- **Learning** - School kept my mind open to new thoughts and discussions. However, typical schooling models do not work well with everyone's learning styles. What's funny is that I'm finding that actions speak louder than words in most situations and no one asks me how many degrees I have or what I have studied. Large corporations still look for credentials but customers want exceptional goods and services. If you have your own business and can satisfy your customer, nothing else matters. Regardless, I do value life-long learning and continue to study many subjects as I deepen my understanding of God and spiritual principles, especially in business.
- **Business** - Good questions to ask before entering any business relationship – Is it the right thing? Is it the right time? Is it the right person?

Generally I am a quick learner, flexible, don't need supervision, and am a very creative multi-tasker who loves people. My sociology studies gave me a broader view of how societies and social settings affect individuals and groups. Mediation taught me many things about keeping centered while staying focused. It also taught me that not all conflict is negative and is, in fact, often an important precursor to growth.

Because I am capable of learning/doing most anything business-related, I haven't always delegated effectively. Sounds like a classic entrepreneur! And delegating to others with their own special expertise is really more beneficial to a company or organization, especially as it grows beyond what an entrepreneur can manage. This is true of any organization – be it a company, a church or a family. All of my education and experiences so far have prepared me to mentor other business leaders and share all that I have learned. With a new partner, that is exactly what I am doing. We have formed a "C" corporation which will act as an incubator for many small businesses and currently provides a family of services:

- **Superior Credit Restoration (SCR)** – credit image reports, credit education and coaching
- **Focused Solutions** – business and leadership coaching/consulting
- **Idotoday.com** – wedding officiant business. How would one know that childhood front porch performances could lead to this! Gentle leading is necessary to help couples design their wedding ceremony. All my years as a family-law mediator will give me an edge in understanding couples considering a long life and future together.

What are the broader lessons for career seekers in the 21st Century? Things have changed since the 60's – from stay-at-home moms to mothers kissing babies goodbye as they run out the door with briefcase in hand. For the better part of the 20th Century, higher education was the path to a successful career. It is still an important credential when seeking a job with a large corporation. However, career jobs are not the tradition any longer. Today's individual looking to set a career in motion (or change careers) will want to review all their strengths and weaknesses, education (traditional or specialized), life experiences, wants and needs, and current economic status. Where the traditional path pointed straight up the corporate ladder, today one needs to be much more flexible and possibly consider multiple tasks or positions. Where does one start when considering the new career landscape?

- First, and foremost, look at what comes naturally. Ask yourself who you are now – not what you are going to be.

- Identify your long term goals.
- Repackage past experience in new or different ways.
- Decide whether additional education/training is necessary.
- Explore what's currently available in the marketplace.

Your long and short-term goals and needs will depend on where you are in age, experience and family life. It may help to write your own story starting from the first memories of who you were in your family (myself first of three girls), transitioning to the main events that held your attention while going through grade school - social events you were involved in, extra-curricular activities (speech competition, drama) - higher education and the disciplines you enjoyed (sociology). Look at each job (paid or not) and identify the running threads. Ask others to give you feedback on how they experience you. When I personally did this exercise, I found I had acquired many different talents throughout my life that can now be used in the current companies. Some were so natural, I took them for granted.

The world is changing, and we must change with it. I challenge you to consider a less traditional career approach. Don't think about what you have lost or might lose. Explore many options. **You** are *the answer*. Keep learning and growing and surround yourself with friends and associates who are doing the same. Look for the emerging opportunities in the current economy.

It's been a Long Road behind Me and a Long Road Ahead

Steve Howard

6

Life, like your career, is a journey. I took that statement to heart, quite literally (and lived to tell about it). I wanted to find my calling – to reconnect with my dormant call to adventure. My journey – an extended road trip – was first described in a journal I began on May 23, 2002, delayed by several months while I taught myself how to write a blog – or more accurately an e-book using "Blogger" when it first came on the market.

Before I tell you about my journey, let's place the starting point in context. It was after the new millennium began, when the dotcom bubble crashed, the earth flattened and the terrorists slammed into the Twin Towers on 9/11. Clearly, a new national chapter was being written. Only we didn't know how it would come out. I wasn't sure how my blog would come out, either. It was a first step, my own personal knowledge laboratory – a pilot experiment designed to continuously learn-as-I-went. Out of it is coming what I'm calling a "Mobile KnowCo" a way for you to live anywhere you want by building "Knowledge ATMs" so you can make money while you sleep without sinking or swimming in the local economy. But, that's another chapter.

Looking back, I might have chosen a different title for my blog – something along the lines of "Confessions of a Boomersaur" or "Removing Boomersaurs from the Endangered Species List." But, instead I chose "The Journal of 2020 Foresight." Later, I added "Reports from the Knowledge Labs about our recent findings, research topics, and interviews with lifestyle leaders who are creating their own futures."

Go ahead. Google the title and you'll find my journal entries posted between 2002 and the end of 2006 in more detail. But for our purposes in this chapter, how can I summarize my lessons learned?

I know.

What if this chapter was a DVD you rented from NetFlix or Blockbuster? What follows would be the bonus behind-the-scenes tracks where the director and actors tell you what it was like working together. Somebody wise, we'll call him Grey Owl, would be conducting the interview. Imagine him asking something, like ….

Grey Owl: Describe the journey in the "Journal of 2020 Foresight" for us the way you (would have) pitched it to a Hollywood studio.

SH: Well … How about: what if Gail Sheehy and Rich Dad piled into an SUV and took a road trip throughout the West? They'd retrace Lewis & Clark's Corps of Discovery. Only this time they're on a journey to find the one restaurant that serves the best bowl of Chicken Soup. They stay for a few days in Telluride during the Film Festival at John Naisbitt's home. Neil Young bums a ride. Reluctantly, they return, having failed in their quest. Except, they have in their possession Mark Twain's recipe. Only they don't know it yet. It's in a trunk they purchased sight unseen at a Virginia City flea market hidden among his letters and unfinished manuscripts. Only the names have been changed. And some of it is true.

Grey Owl: Let's break it down – you took a road trip throughout the West in an SUV?

SH: Yes, true. We drove over 3,000 miles through portions of California, Arizona, Nevada, Colorado and Utah, having hatched the idea sitting on the beach in Cabo San Lucas, Mexico. We picked up the SUV in Sacramento and visited old mining towns in the Sierras like Placerville and Lake Tahoe and backtracked to Oakhurst, Yosemite and attempted to traverse Tioga Pass to Mammoth Mountain -- but, that's another story. We left the Mother Lode and the Comstock Lode country and drove down 395 before heading east. We skirted around Death Valley and the Mojave Desert to stay overnight in Laughlin, Nevada on our way to the Grand Canyon. From there we explored the Mesa Verde Cliff Dwellings and water rafted in Durango before taking the train to Silverton in the San Juan National Forest. From there we lingered in Telluride before heading out to Denver, Boulder and Estes Park. On our way out of Colorado we stayed in Aspen and Vail and then Bryce Canyon before we said goodbye to each other at New York, New York in Vegas and went our separate ways. Phew.

Grey Owl: How do Sheehy and Rich Dad figure in?

SH: With a lesser degree of truthiness, except to say this road trip for us was all about searching for our new American dream, perhaps in small town real estate. We all wanted to see how we could support ourselves if we took the leap and moved to where the environment and quality of life fit our passions. We all realized from our own experiences that what's important at one life stage grows or shrinks in the next. Your passions change and your priorities change. Oh, and since we embarked on a journey of re-discovery and renewal, you can throw in a bowl of Chicken Soup too as soul food, if you want to.

Grey Owl: You picked up a hitchhiking Neil Young?

SH: OK. That gets an even lower rating in truthiness. Actually, we listened to his "Greendale" CD, so he joined us in spirit and lyrics. We found many towns in the West that could have been Greendale –

"Greendale. We're going on a little trip, folks…. So these songs are about a place called Greendale…. There's a lot going on in town. It seems to be a pretty mellow place, really. In town there's about 20 to 25,000 people and it's not a very big place at all "

Oh, and there's one of my favorite songs from his "Prairie Wind" CD

Grey Owl: Let's get to that a little bit later.

SH: OK.

Grey Owl: Why a journey throughout the West in the first place and what's the Lewis & Clark connection?

SH: The Wild West – we were all attracted to the pioneering spirit, resourcefulness and ingenuity. Fierce self-reliance. We admired the capacity to endure hardships. Making do. Living with the pain and suffering. There's something liberating about a journey of adventure with danger lurking around every corner. We discovered later that there's a new vitality – especially when it comes to the emerging alternative energy markets (a complete reversal for states known for natural resource extraction). But we didn't realize that until after we completed the trip. So I'd have to say by virtue of growing up in the Midwest, it seemed like every family takes a vacation out west before the kids leave the nest. That memory came to the forefront as I sifted through some of my dad's things when he passed away a couple of years ago. Two other things clicked as well.

Grey Owl: Like?

SH: On family vacations, we used to visit the small town he grew up in on the Missouri River – up river from St. Louis – the gateway to the West. Quite by coincidence I discovered that Buffalo Bill Cody died in 1917, the year my father was born. So The West was on my mind. And, in my own life, I already had taken Horace Greeley's famous quote seriously – "Go West Young Man." I moved to Southern California, home of the Beach Boys in the '70s.

Grey Owl: You said two things.

SH: Well, at first I was struck by one of the things my dad told me. His first job out of college was selling outhouses. Think how far we had come in his lifetime. Then I read that roughly in one lifetime the Wild West opened starting with the Lewis and Clark expedition 200 years ago between 1804 and 1806 and closed a decade or so before Buffalo Bill Cody passed away in Colorado – so, I focused on what tremendous change had occurred in the span of two lifetimes.

Grey Owl: I sense there is a connection to Mark Twain as well.

SH: It's deeper for me. When I looked at black and white photos of my grandfather I noticed a striking resemblance to Samuel Clemens – Mark Twain. I imagined my father living the Huckleberry Finn or Tom Sawyer childhood along the river. I even had a great uncle who, like Twain, traveled the Missouri River as a river barge captain. Oh, and as it turns out, it was Twain who convinced Buffalo Bill Cody to take his traveling Wild West Show to Europe and perform for the Queen of England.

Grey Owl: How does Virginia City, Nevada fit your pitch to Hollywood?

SH: Quite by accident. Somewhere between Lake Tahoe and Mammoth Mountain the topic of Mono Lake came up. It rang a bell. We had a copy of "Roughing It" by Mark Twain buried with the luggage in the back of the SUV. We found the passage where Twain recalls a misadventure of his at the alkaline lake when his boat drifts away from what looks like a moonscape island he and his partner were exploring. We drove past Mono Lake on California State Highway 395 while reading about his adventure.

Grey Owl: So Twain hung out where you did?

SH: Sure did. He rode a stagecoach all the way from St. Louis to Carson City, Nevada to join his brother Orion, the new secretary to the territorial governor of Nevada. We like to say get-rich schemes and tall tales both consumed and sustained Mark Twain. Shuttling as much as he did between Carson City and Virginia City, it was San Francisco that captured his imagination – but it was Mono Lake that almost killed him – and his curiosity.

Grey Owl: In your modern version of the stagecoach – your SUV – after you traveled through five of eight western states, what lessons did you learn from your journey?

SH: Let me sum it up with a line from Neal Young --"It's Been a Long Road Behind Me, and It's a Long Road Ahead."

Grey Owl: Right. I said we'd come back to him.

SH: First and foremost, take a trip – a real journey. Just like in my college days when we kicked around life's meaning in all night bull sessions, some times you need to revisit core questions like:

Who have I become? What will my life add up to? Do I want to be remembered as the person I have been up to now? Is it too late to put more meaning in my life? Where will I be and what will I be doing in the next five years? Will economic cycles support or defeat my plans? Will I be forced to live a lifestyle I didn't choose or work in a job I hate? Will my energy, vitality and health slowly drain away? As you map out the rest of your journey, which direction will your life take? What kind of legacy do you want to leave?

Grey Owl: Or?

SH: Or, will you re-discover and finally follow your dreams? I like how Neil Young put it in his "Prairie Wind" CD in "The Painter."

The painter stood
Before her work

She looked around everywhere
She saw the pictures and she painted them
She picked the colors from the air
Green to green
Red to red
Yellow to yellow
In the light
Black to black
When the evening comes
Blue to blue
In the night
It's a long road
Behind me
It's a long road
Ahead
If you follow every dream
You might get lost
If you follow every dream
You might
Get Lost.
She towed the line
She held her end up
She did the work of too many
But in the end
She fell down
Before she got up again
I keep my friends eternally
We leave our tracks in the sound
Some of them are with me now
Some of them can't be found
It's a long road behind me
And I miss you now
If you follow every dream
You might get lost
If you follow every dream
You might

Get

Lost.

Grey Owl: Follow your dreams. That's it?

SH: We've all recognized that the rules have changed. It 's no longer enough to simply dream – it's now more about making the best decisions possible in uncertain, confusing times -- whether as individuals, teams or as organizational leaders.

Grey Owl: And?

SH: People have always wanted to know where life will take them. But today we are in one of those periods that occur every 200 or 300 years when people don't understand the world anymore, when the past is not sufficient to explain the future. The turbulent changes and threats in the currents of our lives over the past five years – its pace, pattern and scale – challenge our notions of what is real.

Grey Owl: Is this when John Naisbitt's Mega Trends come in?

SH: Oh, yeah. We skipped right past him, didn't we? I believe that mastering new rules is like trying to cross a white-water river. If you can anticipate the whirlpools and the changes in the current, if you can anticipate the landing on the other shore, you have a much better chance of getting across that river successfully.

Grey Owl: What can we do about our predicament?

SH: When we come to a crossroads in our lives, we can choose any one of 11 options: 1) Change positions in same organization: 2) Change organizations in same field; 3) Change careers; 4) Grow in same job, moonlight; 5) Start a business; 6) Buy a business; 7) Buy a franchise; 8) Develop a consulting practice; 9) Pursue a portfolio career; 10) Live on investment portfolio and volunteer; 11) Retire, yet freelance or consult to supplement income.

Grey Owl: What if you pick one of those but all the jobs go off shore, for instance? Or your employer is acquired. Or we encounter a major recession? Or …

SH: That's always a possibility – perhaps a probability these days. So, you want to take educated guesses when choosing. Which option(s) will current markets and longer-term future trends support? Which ones will lead to dead ends and disappointment?

Grey Owl: What you're really talking about is looking at your career as an investment in your life's portfolio.

SH: That's right. We're looking at 3 to 5 year windows – like angel investors do for their return on investment. Will economic cycles before and after 2010 – 2012 support your plans?

Grey Owl: As you grow through succeeding life stages your interests change as you re-balance your priorities, don't they?

SH: You have to always improve. Stay up-to-date with advances in your profession. Remain marketable. Find the right fit for your stage in life, in the right community, doing what you are passionate about, in the right kind of organization at the right stage of development.

Grey Owl: Your career is one thing, what about the community in which you live and your personal life?

SH: Our trip, we said earlier, was about finding our version of the American dream. We looked for Greendale. What is yours? If you're like us, will you be doing what you love while living your own version of the new American Dream in a resort town, small college and university town, classic town, revitalized factory towns, exurb, suburban village, emerging new city, large-growth city, or urban village?

Grey Owl: But, you have to take the first step to find out.

SH: And the second and third. Which reminds me. As hard as it is to boil down all the wisdom I've acquired throughout the years into one chapter, I believe Portia Nelson did it for me in her poem, "Autobiography in Five Short

Chapters," from her book, *There's A Hole in My Sidewalk.*

I

I walk, down the street.
There is a deep hole in the sidewalk.
I fall in
I am lost ... I am helpless
It is my fault.
It takes forever to find a way out.

II

I walk down the same street.
There is a deep hole in the sidewalk.
I pretend I don't see it.
I fall in again.
I can't believe I am in the same place,
But it isn't my fault.
It still takes a long time to get out.

III

I walk, down the street.
There is a deep hole in the sidewalk.
I see it is there.
I still fall in ... it's a habit
My eyes are open.
I know where I am.
It is my fault.
I get out immediately.

IV

I walk down the same street.
There is a deep hole in the sidewalk.
I walk around it.

V

I walk down another street.

We return you now to your regularly scheduled program.

Life Begins at 50 – or Whatever Age You Choose

Rochelle Burgess

7

"You are not at the top of your game anymore," the Chief Financial Officer said to the HR Manager of a Fortune 500 company' small division. She asked, "Is it time for a change?" The HR manager was me, and the CFO was right. I loved my chosen profession. Yet I had successfully faked my enthusiasm for and dedication to a corporate career for several years, and had finally reached the point where I could no longer keep up the façade. I was tired, frustrated, disillusioned with the corporate environment and ready to make a change. How large a change could I make? After thirty years as a Human Resources professional with only three companies on my resume, what change could possibly make a difference in my energy level and ability to succeed? The only change available, in my own mind was to leave the company and find smaller organizations that could utilize and appreciate my unique strengths.

I was acknowledged as a coach and mentor to individual managers and employees. My internal clients also respected my knowledge of Human Resources. Still, I was fearful of my own potential shortcomings. Would I have the self-confidence and the stamina to succeed? Could I become organized enough? Could I overcome my procrastination? Could I manage change myself as successfully as the classes I taught on managing change?

The dilemma, then, was: how would a single woman with my entire career centered on Leadership Development and Human Resources be able to make a mid-life career change. I cared passionately about these fields and about my clients. I decided to start my own consulting business. That decision felt absolutely right on an emotional level. Yet how would I survive financially outside the corporate structure that had sustained me for thirty years with all my strengths and weaknesses?

As I thought about the path that had brought me to this traumatic and drastic decision point, I realized that my strength would come from two life changing experiences, just a few years before – going back to school and the death of my grandmother. Feeling stale in my profession and my personal life, I had enrolled in a Masters Degree program and after three years of taking one class at a time, I received the degree from Chapman University in Organizational Leadership. The very last class of the entire program occurred on my 50th birthday, exactly 30 years after receiving my Bachelor's degree in Education from the University of Michigan.

The master's degree program forced me to keep current on political and business community events. It forced me to research effective leadership strategies and to write papers analyzing my corporate employer, making recommendations for action and offering potential solutions to business issues. I had to practice what I learned, both in the classroom and back at the office. A new confidence emerged in my own ability as a consultant to senior management.

Then, in a class titled "Leadership & Team Development," I participated in a weekend of experiential learning that included an exercise on the high ropes. Packed into a belay, harness and helmet, we climbed 30 feet into the air on a rope ladder and then walked across wires suspended between trees. At the end of the exercise we took a leap of faith off of a platform and jumped toward a trapeze. Then each of us was lowered slowly to the ground. After my total terror of climbing the rope ladder and walking across the wires, I felt like a very mellow Tinker Bell from the Peter Pan story, floating back down to solid land. To my surprise, I could not wait to try it again! For myself, many of my classmates, and now many of my students over the past eight years, the feeling was, "If I can accomplish this, I can truly survive and accomplish anything the business organization throws at me."

I remained involved with Chapman's leadership program, particularly the team building classes, and within two years became an adjunct professor teaching that same class at the graduate and undergraduate level along with research classes in which students write the equivalent of a short doctoral dissertation. My enthusiasm for teaching became much more compelling than my corporate job. I did not realize at the time that I was already starting to change my career direction. I still continue to watch my adult students develop a new self-confidence and increased self-esteem, as they accomplish initiatives in my classes that "wow" senior management in their places of work.

The second life changing experience occurred just prior to leaving the corporate life. I returned to my home town of Detroit to attend my grandmother's funeral. During that visit, the four generations of our family reminisced about our memories of the 104-year-old matriarch, or "bubby" as she was called. A nephew, then in his thirties, told us that he was embarrassed to admit he was her favorite of all the grandchildren and great-grandchildren. One of my older brothers responded, "There was never any question that I was clearly her favorite." Of course, I chimed in with, "There was never a doubt in my mind that I was her favorite." Around the table we went, each one of 17 family members insisting we were the favorite child.

At that moment I realized this woman had such a capacity to make each of us – her clients – feel so special just by listening to each person, anticipating his needs and providing her sincere and loving attention, that each felt certain he or she was the most important customer. I took that concept into my own consulting business. In fact, I tell most of my clients and my audiences the grandmother story because it gets attention when we are discussing the significance of internal and external customer service. One of my clients told me she had repeated the story to another business owner who then became a client. I smiled and silently thanked my grandmother for her inspiration.

My consulting business is now in its seventh year and I've become a speaker on HR and leadership topics. I conduct management and leadership training with small companies and divisions of larger companies. I have learned so much about so many different industries, and I enjoy being a business partner to my clients. My clients are all referrals from other colleagues or companies I have met through networking. Most of my earlier clients are still with me and continue to refer my services to others. My teaching career has come full circle, from a B.A. degree in secondary education to becoming a college professor.

A significant accomplishment early in my new career was learning how to network. I became active in a professional coaches' group, an HR association and a women business owners' organization. Each one offered opportunities not so much for clients, but for partnering in projects and referrals to clients. Without planning it, I developed a reputation as a "connector," the person who could introduce anyone to someone else who might help them. That turned out to be so much more powerful than trying to "sell" my services!

While I earned less net income until recently than I did in my former job, I would not trade my quality of life for one heartbeat. My friends in former companies are often impressed and envious that I have successfully earned a living outside the confines of a large company. My clients appreciate my unique strengths, such as helping them resolve crisis situations and keeping their companies legally sound. While I have always been a procrastinator and somewhat disorganized, these challenges are more easily managed since most client needs are immediate.

I still work sixty to seventy hours each week, as I did in the corporate world; yet, being able to choose which 60-70 hours is a source of satisfaction for me. My passion is for my clients' success on the people side of their business and my intent is to make each business owner feel as though he or she is my most important client. My first attempts were finding corporate clients. Once I realized my niche was small to mid-size business owners, I was off and running!

My advice to individuals who are considering mid-life career changes from corporate to consulting is fourfold: (a) Identify your passion and your strengths: build on those areas you are truly passionate about and find your "niche" clients; (b) Don't procrastinate: have a business plan if at all possible, but start our business even without one; (c) Get organized with your resources: be frugal in your personal spending yet don't be afraid to invest in the hardware, software, or association memberships needed in order to get your business off to a fast start.

My new career, and my new life, began at age 50 – when will yours start?

"I probably hold the distinction of being the one movie star who, by all the laws of logic, should never have made it. At each stage of my career, I lacked the experience."

Audrey Hepburn
1929-1993
American Actress

Take Charge of Your Career 8

Lee Pound

I've spent most of my life doing things most people would never attempt without thorough training.

Such as becoming a newspaper editor with only six months full time experience, taking a chief financial officer job with no formal accounting experience, writing novels and non-fiction books, speaking to large groups with no training in speaking skills, and putting on a world-class seminar for speakers with no previous seminar experience.

If it sounds like I'm nuts or crazy, think again. Many great achievers made their first splash as complete novices. They had an idea and they followed it wherever it took them. Many succeeded beyond their wildest dreams.

Then there is everyone else, the perpetual students who are never quite ready to act, who take class after class and find guru after guru, only to end up empty-handed. Meanwhile, they work at some boring job in corporate America wishing they could do what they really want to do. Pretty soon the job defines who they are and traps them for years.

It doesn't have to be like this.

It doesn't take years of training to be a success. It takes action. It takes a willingness to risk failure. It takes a

57

willingness to risk rejection. For instance, the only way to write a book is to start writing, submit it to an editor, take the bad news and go back and rewrite. In all areas of life, if you never hear criticism, you're not risking enough.

You see, I never fell for the corporate America trap. And yes, I never had the fancy office 50 stories up, the limousine, the power sports car, the big boss yelling at me, the 20-hour days or week-long business trips, office politics, and the lack of satisfaction.

I worked for smaller companies. I learned every aspect of how a business runs, how to write news stories, design newspaper pages, give speeches to large crowds, write fiction, write non-fiction, tell stories, work with shareholders and board members of a public corporation, coach and edit writers, hire and fire employees. I even took acting classes. All because I wanted to, not because I had to.

What does this mean for you?

Let's say you're stuck in a job you don't like, trying to start a business but can't get clients, want to speak or write a book to help grow your business and present you as an expert but don't know how, think its too hard to make a business work, too hard, too hard, too hard.

Wouldn't you want to follow the example of a coach who's done all this, an editor who actually knows how to edit, a writer who learned writing from one of the most respected book publishers of the 20th Century, and a speech coach who has 30 years experience and actually puts on high level programs for speakers?

Of course. And you can.

But, I'm sure you're asking, how could I have done all that? That's too many careers that don't work together. Too many skills I'd have to spend years learning.

And you'd be right. In most cases. I just don't think that way. It isn't the training that matters. Taking action matters, even if you fall on your face a few times. I grabbed opportunities and then figured out how to do them.

Here's exactly how I did it. And how you can do it too.

What about the seminar business, *Speak Your Way to Wealth*? How did that happen?

It happened for one simple reason. I was open to an opportunity. *Speak Your Way to Wealth* happened because I walked out the door of a marketing seminar with a friend, Arvee Robinson, who became my business partner, and we agreed we could put on a seminar for speakers. A big one. We knew nothing about the business. We simply set a goal, a vision, and pursued it relentlessly. We asked experts when we needed information; we hired the best help we could find, asked nationally ranked speakers to appear, and made it happen.

Speaking in Public, the Number One Ranked Fear

I never intended to be a speaker. In fact I might never have spoken in public except for one incident. It wasn't fear. I simply didn't know you were supposed to be afraid. Among other things I am a family historian. Over thirty years ago I found some ancestors in Germany, very difficult to do, and mentioned it at my Genealogy Society. The program chairman asked me to give a speech on how I did it at the next meeting.

In front of 150 people. For one hour.

And like a fool, I said yes, gave the speech, and started a thirty-year speaking career without even thinking about it.

Writing Fiction, Everyone's "Want To Do but Never Get around To" Dream

Okay, it was mine too, for years. But one day, soon after I got a computer, an idea I'd kicked around for years suddenly wanted out and I wrote, for six weeks, every evening, typing,

typing, typing. And when I was done I had a novel, 680 pages worth.

So I showed it to a friend. And reality hit. I have to admit I wanted praise and never expected her answer, which was, "You should take a class in writing fiction."

I decided I needed a mentor. Getting a good one is tough. You may never work with the best in your line of business. Whoever you work with, you will find him or her in the place you least expect. You must be ready when the opportunity presents itself.

I went to writing conferences, classes and writers groups, met writing teachers, other writers, conference leaders and made many new friends. My writing skills gradually improved and in the fall of 1989 I started a new novel.

A few months later, the UC Irvine Extension class schedule arrived in the mail. I glanced at it and set it aside. A few days later I noticed it on my desk under a pile of papers and opened it to the writing section. I took one final glance at the writing classes and noticed one on dialogue. The teacher was Sol Stein. The name was vaguely familiar. I read his bio. Owner of Stein & Day Publishers in New York. Who could pass up learning from one of the premier publishers of the twentieth century?

I signed up. Ten weeks later, after one of the most breathtakingly excellent classes I had ever experienced, the forty members of the class asked this question: *What do we do now?* Sol Stein responded with a proposition. He would set up a small seminar, about 15 members, which would meet in his living room in Laguna Beach for ten Monday nights every winter and study writing. *"Send me the first three pages of your book,"* he said, *"and I will tell you if you are in or out."*

That's how I learned story skills.

In four years of sitting in Sol Stein's living room in Laguna Beach, I learned to write in ways I had only imagined possible. Sol featured one chapter from my novel *A Gathering of Strangers* in his video program, *Stein on Writing,* filmed in a house overlooking the Pacific Ocean in Corona del Mar, California. Imagine my excitement, sitting beside Sol Stein, discussing my chapter and having it used as an example of how to do it right. What a thrill!

What about that chief financial officer job. Where does that fit in?

Surprised that I went from editor to CFO? I thought so. Most people are. Most editors are congenitally unable to do numbers much less operate at such a high level in the financial field. Wouldn't you want to learn writing from someone who understood your business as well as writing skills? Of course you would. And of course you know how hard such a person is to find.

Over those twenty years, I made payrolls, paid bills, managed salespeople, editors, and other managers. I have seen rapid sales growth and I have managed financial difficulties, including taking three corporations through a successful Chapter 11 bankruptcy, a feat so difficult that ninety percent of companies fail when they try it.

I watched employees work, listened to their problems, observed several successful sales people and many others who failed. I watched managers lead well and lead poorly.

"Wait a minute," you ask. "How did you go from editor to chief financial officer? Don't you need special training for that?"

Yes and no. If you know how to learn when the opportunity arises, if you know how to plant the seeds with the decision makers, if you are willing to take advantage of an opportunity at which you may fail, then no, you do not need special training.

And that's what happened. The opportunity arose. I took it and figured out how to do it later. I became chief financial officer of a public corporation ten days before the 10-Q was due. I had no idea what a 10-Q was or that it was due. I discovered that a 10-Q was a document required by the federal Securities and Exchange Commission and that not filing it was not an option. So I figured out how to do it and did it. A few months later I managed an audit by Ernst & Whinney, then one of the top eight accounting firms in the world, working with people who audited Fortune 500 corporations. And I came through it with very few changes to my financials.

I have one more secret that can help you take your business to a new level, a level you never dreamed possible. And what might that be? After all, I'm a writer and a chief financial officer, both occupations usually filled by introverts. What else can I bring to the table? So here it is, the last secret:

You don't need fancy training. You don't need years of experience. You simply need to tell yourself a different story about what you want and how you will get it.

As you can see, I thought in a way that brought opportunity. I told myself a story that was so vivid I could believe it and make it happen, every time.

Over the Niagara Falls of Life 9

James Richards

C an a person survive a life-changing crisis and come back smiling?

Crisis:
   a. A crucial or decisive point or situation; a turning point.
   b. An unstable condition, as in political, social, or economic affairs, involving an impending abrupt or decisive change.
   c. An emotionally stressful event or traumatic change in a person's life. (American Heritage Dictionary)

The Beginning of the End
The icy hand of fear gripped my mind as I realized that the last of my assets were now gone. The last few weeks had been horrific -- asset after asset, property after property and investment after investment being sold to pay debts that seemed to grow by the hour.

Now I had nothing left to show for twenty years of hard work building a multi-million dollar net worth. What had taken half of my working life to develop had disappeared in less than a month. I was broke, unemployed and had just moved into a rented house. To make matters worse, I had no idea how the next month's rent would be paid. All I could see ahead of me was struggle, poverty and misery.

It was 1987 – a banner year for my business and the year our advisors helped us become listed on the Stock Market. This was the big pay-off year when millions of shares in our business would climb to a price that would enable us to live in luxury for the rest of our lives.

But even the smartest of our advisors didn't reckon on Black Friday in October 1987 when share prices on stock exchanges all around the world crashed. Stock in my well-established corporation had been floated a few weeks earlier and the resultant collapse in stock price set up the chain-reaction – I call it the domino effect – that led to my dramatic reversal of fortune.

It seemed that every negative emotion possible now swept over me – shame, humiliation, guilt, anger, and fear haunted my every waking moment. Things that I had taken for granted now became big issues in my life. I kept asking myself, "How do I feed my family?" "Will I be able to get a job?" "Where do I go from here?"

Sure, I had experienced tough times in my business career but nothing could have prepared me for this traumatic, mind-numbing reversal of my life situation. Wealth had been exchanged for poverty, security for insecurity, confidence for fear and raw optimism for hopelessness.

The final ignominy came when my attorney advised me to declare bankruptcy. He said, "Your assets are all gone and you have nothing left to pay any further bills." The next morning we filed Chapter 7 in the courthouse and with this formality, a 20-year run of success came to a screeching halt.

Was it just a few weeks earlier that I had stood on the beach contentedly watching the waves from the Pacific Ocean come crashing at my feet? Our architecturally designed, luxury beach-front home with its 180 degree ocean views was just a few yards behind me and my children enjoyed the surf while my wife kept a motherly eye on them. Nothing could have been more perfect. I was happy, contented and confident and there was no thought in my mind of anything other than future success.

Let me tell you quite definitely - it was wonderful being a successful businessman. My wife and I enjoyed beautiful homes, world travel, prestigious events, fine dining, and private schools. We even owned two ranches, a dairy herd, and orchards. Of course we drove the very best automobiles and would never consider flying any other way than first class. It had been a long time since we had stopped to work out the price of anything we wanted to buy. If we wanted it, we bought it. Yes, it was a good feeling to have reached the top and to be in a position to enjoy the very best that the world could offer.

How could everything have gone so wrong so quickly? My mind flitted over the past month but it was just a blur in my mind. Perhaps I was dreaming. Yes! That was it – this was just a nightmare and I would soon awaken to find everything back to its comfortable normalcy.

My reverie came back to reality as I realized that this was no dream that I would gently awake from. It was a nightmare all right but it was happening in real time to my family and me. Was there no hope?

These runaway thoughts were interrupted when my wife, Yvonne, said to me, "James, when we first got married, we had nothing. Together we built a wonderful life. I firmly believe that together we can do it again." Then she added, "It's not all about money, you know. We have a great marriage; three wonderful sons and we live in a country that still offers opportunity to those that work hard. And you are a hard worker."

This was the first ray of hope that touched me and I thought, "Maybe I can shake off the negative emotions that are crippling me and stopping me from thinking anything other than gloom and despair. Is there a future for me out there somewhere?" I hugged my wife and decided there and then to start a new chapter in my life – one that was going to have a much better ending than the one just concluded.

Over the next few months I started to rebuild my future. I knew the most important step I could make was to develop new skills to enable me to face up to and overcome this overwhelming crisis. I discovered that many people have to face crises in their lives - some financial like mine - others health, divorce, family, career, addictions, and more. Every day thousands of unfortunate people smash into their personal brick walls and don't know how to handle it.

As a result of my experiences, I was forced to develop tools to enable me to cope with this massive crisis in my life and somehow come back smiling. Perhaps you are going through a crisis in your life now. In this limited space let me share with you one of the tools that helped me become happy, content and confident once again, this time on a much sounder and realistic foundation.

This is one game you don't want to play.

I learned a valuable lesson from someone else who had gone through the most terrible of times. He was fabulously wealthy – a very successful man. Unexpectedly, he too lost everything. His wife and ten children died, his assets were stolen, his employees were murdered, he lost all his wealth, and to make matters worse he became very ill. In a very short time he went from being a very happy, successful and wealthy man living on his estate in Uz, to become a poverty-stricken, invalid widower.

What did I learn from Job? (Yes, it is Job from the Bible I am talking about). I learned that when adversity strikes – don't play the "Blame Game." Oh, it was so tempting to lash out with a bitter tongue to blame all those that hurt me, led me astray, wouldn't help or were indifferent to my problems. But what would this achieve? Realistically, it wouldn't hurt anyone accept myself, and at a time like this when I was hurting so much already, why would I want to add to my misery?

Job, in spite of all his problems, didn't blame God as his friends thought he would. Because he had the right attitude, he was eventually restored to an even greater position than he had originally. Was he glad that he had all these trials? Of course not, but by not becoming bitter and pointing the finger of blame, he made himself a good candidate for rehabilitation to a prosperous and fruitful life.

I am so glad that my wife and I made the decision soon after the collapse of our business ventures not to play the "Blame Game." I have seen others who have fallen into this trap and have become embittered, empty and old before their time. It is very easy to blame everyone else for your misfortunes but it achieves nothing except frustration and angst.

Play the "Blame Game" and you will never get over the effects of your crisis. You will relive it over and over again. You will keep experiencing the hurts, the pain and the failure for the rest of your life.

Accept responsibility and you will experience a cleansing of your spirit, a stiffening of your resolve and a quickening of your determination to overcome the crisis that has so wounded you. So thank you, Job, for teaching me that even in the darkest period of my life, I will never play the "Blame Game."

The Second Time Around

How foolish I was to think that I could re-build my life in just a few months or a couple of years. Do you remember the tragic collapse of the World Trade Center in New York following the terrorist attack? The decision to rebuild was made quickly but it took several years just to take away the debris so that a smooth foundational base could be created. Then before re-construction could commence, there was a period of planning followed by further months of challenges that needed to be overcome. The collapse of a life is no different and the bigger the crisis, the longer it takes to clear away the debris so a fresh start can be constructed onto a sound foundation. Re-building your life on a base that is littered with garbage and problems is not a good idea.

In my case, it took me five years to deal with the aftershocks of our business and financial collapse. During this time I had to re-think every part of my life and how I wanted to live in the future. I decided that I did not want to be a business tycoon again. The money was great but the pressure was even greater. Nor did I want to work for an employer. I had been independent for far too long. The answer was to start a small family business where I could enjoy the maximum amount of time working with my wife and sons and have some spare time to pursue my new interests.

One major benefit of my crisis is that it forced me to face up to my own mortality and to ask what many before have asked, "What is the meaning of my life?" I came to the conclusion that my earlier pursuit of money and power was rather meaningless and shallow when measured against the history of mankind and the awesome majesty of Creation. It was during this period that I found God – or should I say, He found me. Instantly my life and its purpose came into clear focus as I started to understand the level of satisfaction and fulfillment that comes from being involved with causes greater than oneself.

It would be fair to say that the emphasis in my life until then had been on my career and success. Now I also focused on helping others help themselves. The very crisis that had engulfed me had also equipped me to help others in even worse situations than mine.

Dr. Robert H. Schuller tells us that when recovering from personal disaster we can create a benefit from our bad experience by "Turning our Scars into Stars." Albeit unwillingly, I had gained experience in disaster and crisis management that would make me a very useful guide to others following the same slippery path to the bottom. In the past few years I have helped countless others overcome their problems and rebuild their lives on a solid foundation.

While continuing to work in our family business, I spent my spare time studying for the ministry and eventually was ordained as a pastor at the world famous Crystal Cathedral in California. My wife and I are involved there in leadership capacities as volunteers, and I have become very active in missionary work, starting new churches and schools in other countries. I have also started and run an online seminary for student pastors in Asia. All this is only possible through the wonders of the Internet. I am able to teach all over the world without leaving California and without my students leaving their home countries.

I used to have hundreds of employees who called me "Boss" and worked very hard for my benefit. Now I have hundreds of student pastors and church members who call me "Pastor and Teacher," and I work hard for their benefit. My workload has never been so heavy but paradoxically, it has never been so light. The difference is that when we become involved in a cause greater than ourselves, we become energized by our work rather than exhausted. It may be difficult to understand, but the new direction I am now following has given me a life that is rewarding beyond anything that I experienced in my old life.

Am I pleased that I lost all my worldly possessions and had to start from the bottom again? The answer is a resounding no! But I am very happy that in spite of my experience, my life has become fulfilling and meaningful to a degree that I could never have conceived in my earlier years.

Yes, I plunged head first over the Niagara Falls of Life, was crushed and beaten to a standstill, but I not only survived to tell the tale, I've also come back smiling.

Section Two

Wisdom and Strategies

"Your work is to discover your work and then with all your heart give yourself to it."

Gautama Buddha
c 540-460 BC
Founder of Buddhism

Finding a New Career   10

Steve Amos

Most of us don't know how to find a new career. We just look for a job similar to the one we had. After all it used to make us a good living. However, that job is gone because of the economy, time, technology, age, or change. Is it time to find a new career? Where do you start?

First know thyself.

Ask yourself this question: "What do I do well?" You'll have dozens of answers. We are children of God with many gifts that we take for granted.

Make a list. Include everything you are good at:
- Closing deals
- Filing quarterly 10-K reports
- Organizing data
- Catching a ball
- Finding the root causes of problems
- Balancing a quarter on your nose
- Marketing products
- Finding the perfect dress
- Putting the right team together
- Blocking volleyballs

Write down everything. Sports, shopping, hobbies, and charities can show you are good at more than your old job. Keep expanding the list. How many can you think of?

Next write down all your successes.
This is not what other people think are your successes. It is anything you did that you felt was a success. What are you proud of? What successes did you have at work? What accomplishments are you happy with? What was a success in school? What have you done outside work? Remember different times in your life from school, college, and jobs. Every two to five years you probably had a success, maybe several in the same year. How many can you remember?

Are you impressed? Look at the skills you have learned.

What did you want to be as a kid?
Soldier? Fireman? Doctor? Nurse? Architect? All are great positions. Figure why you wanted to be in that field: Were you trying to make mom proud? Earn a lot of money? Did you want to protect people? These answers will give you clues about your true desires.

I wanted to be a race car driver, fly a plane, and own a store like my grandfather. I like to control my career. That is why I am drawn to entrepreneurial companies and volunteer to use my best skills. I like to control my priorities and contribute more than expected. How many of your childhood desires still speak to you today?

What problems can you solve?
Employers hire for one of three reasons, to make money, save money or solve a problem. Make or save more than you cost and you have the job. We all need to be problem solvers.

Make a list of the problems you can solve. Cheat from all the lists you have made so far. Add two or three per day. Add more. The further you get the better you know yourself.

How You Can Help

Next, tell people how you can help them by using your accomplishments. Create stories. If I did this for them, I can do it for you. The format is called PAR: problem, action, and result. Describe the problem you or your company faced. How did it affect the business? Would you have lost the customer? Can you image the consequences?

Next, tell what actions you took. If you did not do it by yourself, take credit for your contributions. A career search is not the time for false modesty or for taking credit for the work others did. Be specific about what you did. Did you see a need others missed? Create a new service or product? Expedite processes to meet a deadline. Solve a quality problem? Think!

Write down the results. Did you save the day? Keep the customer satisfied? What happened after your action?

What would the problem have cost if you hadn't solved it? How much did productivity improve? How many people did you help? Quantify your results to tell your story even better.

Use the PAR as you tell your story. Say each one out loud. Tell problem – action - results to your family and friends. Change the order as you tell them. In advertising you have 30 seconds to make your point. Answer different questions by telling the stories in different ways. Begin with the results then summarize the problem and action taken. The result creates enough interest that they will listen to rest of the story.

You should be proud of yourself by now. Ask yourself what personal qualities and abilities have gotten you to where you are? How could you apply those qualities and abilities to starting and building a new business? Answer these and you know the values that give you purpose.

Do your research.

Look at these lists of skills, problems solved, and accomplishments. Figure out what positions you can perform well in. How many ways can you use your skills? See what other ways you can serve humanity, not just making money. Do you have a purpose in helping others? Most of us will create a list of different job titles. Find as many new careers or job titles as you can and decide whether they need your skills.

Research these job titles. Is there demand? Do they need consultants? Can you work from where you live? Do you have to move? If you don't want to move go further down the list. Next you have to find out how much each job pays. If it does not pay much, you may have to research further. For instance, a hair stylist does not make a lot of money but the salon owners who rent space to hair stylists make commissions on their earnings. How else can you leverage your skills? Find other successful business people and find out how they succeeded. Learn from their mistakes and successes. Often they will help their competitors because they are not afraid to grow. They may even need you to handle their overloads. Your own business is a lot of work and very rewarding if you desire it.

Choose your career.

Don't pick a career just for the money. Which jobs do you care about? What job would you get up early to do? Who do you really want to serve? The more you care the better you will do. You will study harder, practice more, and give extra effort. One percent more effort than your competitors will differentiate you from the crowd.

Odds are we will change our priorities as we grow. Do not be afraid to do this exercise every time you want to grow. You may be surprised where you go as you get older. I never intended to speak or write. I never intended to leave my hometown and work all across the United States. But I would not give it up for all I learned and the wonderful people I have met. See if you don't grow more than you expect.

Why Careers are like Real Estate Markets

Steve Howard

11

ere's what I learned the hard way.

The best career advice usually starts with describing your passions. You take personality assessments. Then you carefully craft a plan capitalizing on your personality type. In theory you make career or business decisions based on doing what you love.

I'm here to tell you that that's only part of what you have to do. You can't just consider your own needs in the current stage of your life cycle when you plan the key events of your life. Economic life cycles can and will have a major impact on those decisions.

Why? Careers are like real estate investments. They appreciate in value in up economies and depreciate in downturns. Real estate cycles can last from a few years to a decade in length. A typical five-year up real estate cycle shifts after prices have increased 30% to 60% before peaking. The downturn ranges from 10% to 40%.

The same can be said about your career. Guess right and you will prosper handsomely. Guess wrong and you might be out on the street. If you don't continuously upgrade your skills, knowledge, and abilities, your equity (your perceived value and marketability) will tank.

The probability that you will be sold in a seller's (employer's) market increases if you aren't paying attention to shifting trends in the real world that force employers to cut back, re-structure or become acquired. Your value to a new employer may drop 40% as well. You may be on the market longer than you want.

It doesn't have to be that way if you adopt what I call a strategic career investment viewpoint.

Real estate investors monitor seven indicators when they decide to buy, sell or hold a property.

Investors plan to buy low, ride an appreciation rocket and sell high. How do they decide when the timing is right to make a profit or avoid a loss?

They monitor clues. They make educated guesses by tracking a set of trends – shifting inflation rates, interest rates, the flow of funds, job growth rates, migration rates and the rate and path of new development.

Companies use the same strategy as a real estate investor when it comes to their talent portfolio. They react to industry and consumer shifts and they ask whether they should buy, sell, or hold.

Your current or last employer forecasts how those shifts play out in strategic planning sessions using a version of the SWOT analysis – Strengths, Weaknesses, Opportunities, and Threats - as they brainstorm the impact of STEEP: Social, Technological, Economic, Environmental, and Political trends.

Not everyone is included in decisions that flow from the analysis. Frequently pink slips get distributed with little or no prior warning.

Those of us who have been in transition can tell you that when you are blind-sided it's not fun. Major disruptions in our lives force us to change our normal habits.

A widespread and prolonged economic disruption across industries may dictate where and how you retire, the value of your house, where you live, your children's education and career choices, your hobbies, whether your are starting, buying, or selling a business, your estate and tax planning, and even your charitable giving.

We know from change experts that we respond to a job loss in one of two ways. The first is a version of walking the plank. We're pushed off a cliff into the valley of despair.

Through selective filtering prior to the pink slip, we miss the clues that suggest just how close we've come to the edge of the cliff or plank. Then we're falling through space.

The second is a process of anticipation. The first drains all of your energy. The second feels more like an adventure.

If only they gave you enough advanced warning to avoid the trauma.

If you received advanced warnings and acted on the potential threat, you would have activated a career, job search, or business plan months before the event. Because it's very rare to get any kind of warning, you have to anticipate and adapt on your own.

In the real world, you need to become your own strategic planning department to see the writing on the wall. Having walked the plank enough times, here are seven steps you can take to prosper from my experience while enjoying your new adventure:

1. State the specific decision to be made -- begin with a decision or plan first.

It might be a variation of these two:

"At this point in my life I only want to follow my passion and do what I love – even if it means I move to another town or city."

Or, "Given my degree of marketability, I want my next job

to be the best fit for me that I can find."

2. Identify the major environmental forces likely to impact the decision.

For answering my passionate calling, ten trends in technology, real estate, economic forecasts, and demographic migration patterns dominated my list. I considered economic bubbles bursting, the Internet reaching 90% household penetration to vacation-home-buying baby boomers, and broad migrations to the west and southeastern portions of the US.

For another project, I facilitated a human resources task force that listed 19 trends out of 100 that they felt would impact the composition of employees in companies of the future. They evaluated generation X, Y, and Z demographics together with baby boomer statistics. They considered the increase in free agent preferences and globalization with new technologies including alternative energy.

3. Develop four plausible and qualitatively different possibilities for each force.

Here's the problem with scenarios. Usually we choose three – the best case, worst case, and a third case, which we call the probable, somewhere in the middle. Then we focus on the probable scenario to the exclusion of the other two, which defeats our purpose.

No one can predict the future. All we want to do is identify contingency plans to prevent disastrous results. Take 9/11. The event shocked all of us because no one believed it could happen here, even though the signals had been mounting months ahead of time.

Being human, we selectively filter out distractions and filter in information we think is important. Our experience and belief system governs those filters. What we filter out can actually do us a lot of harm.

But, by forcing ourselves to construct four different future scenarios, we stretch our perspective and by-pass our selective filters to other possibilities. We don't want to make a decision to invest a lot of time, money and energy into a new business only to overlook a fatal flaw that makes the enterprise unfeasible from the beginning.

For instance, following our passions and earning a living at it normally hinges on the demand for it in the local community within a reasonable driving radius. If you plan to move for higher quality-of-life reasons to a new neighborhood in a different state, you have to answer a whole host of questions. Can you still earn a living if the local economy doesn't support your venture? What if the town's people reject you as an outsider? Is there a way you can win them over? Or will you give up after a short time and move back? Is it possible to enjoy a new lifestyle and make money while you sleep?

4. Assemble the alternatives into internally consistent stories.

My list of ten trends for supporting or short-circuiting a passion-filled life fell roughly along two dimensions – "Doing What You Love vs. Doing What You Hate" and "Living in the Same Geographical Location vs. Moving to a New Preferred Community."

Our human resources taskforce defined four future cultures, the types of talented people who would be attracted to them and retained as valuable contributors. Knowing more about those talent cultures helps job seekers and career changers who are searching for the best fit tremendously.

Their nineteen trends revealed two different dimensions as well – "Independent Identity vs. Organizational Affiliation" and "Technology-Driven Speed vs. Time for Mastery."

5. Tell four different stories about how each scenario

unfolds as if you were a reporter looking back from the future.

The fun part of this step is to describe four uniquely different screenplays or documentaries. Each starts with the same original trends but concludes with four extremely different endings.

My passion and location scenarios described four different communities in which to follow your dreams: "Wealthy Influentials," "Wireless Resorters," "High Country Eagles," and "Permanently Temporary Boomersaurs."

Permanently Temporary Boomersaurs don't anticipate the future and have a hard time adapting to new work realities. Many become consultants and entrepreneurs because they can't find full-time employment. They aspire to become **Wealthy Influentials**, but when forced to move for lower cost of living opportunities choose small university towns populated with **High Country Eagles** in higher quality-of-life communities. They long for face-to-face project-based work as a way of affiliating with other people on a more regular basis and as a way to demonstrate their value in a new organization. They miss the teamwork and seek to counterbalance the isolation and extreme independence they are forced to endure now that they are on their own – no matter if they are interim middle managers, trapped urbanites or just starting over.

Wealthy Influentials live in neighborhoods enjoying the affluently elite American dream. It's as if they've cornered a wealth-generating system. They find a safe haven for high margin income, pay for a high cost of living, accumulate peak real estate appreciation, and live in a secluded, secure, and mature community. Selling products or services to this group means offering highly personalized, luxury, and one-of-a-kind experiences.

Wireless Resorters share the love of a new quality-of-life community with **High Country Eagles.** With the ability to operate anywhere there is Internet access, anyone can move to smaller towns and rural regions.

Examples of each of the four futures abound across the western region of the United States: **Wealthy Influential** neighborhoods like Del Mar or Coronado in California; **High Country Eagle** towns like Sedona or Bisbee in Arizona or Angel Fire and Taos in New Mexico; **Permanently Trapped Boomersaur** parts of Reno, Nevada or Coeur d'Alene, Idaho; or, some of the better know ski resorts fitting the **Wireless Resorters** like Breckenridge and Steamboat Springs in Colorado.

6. Identify hidden opportunities or threats to your future plans.

If you're looking for the best employer for you, the culture fitness scenarios describe four different types of work arrangements that attract distinct talent clusters: "Paradoxy-Morons," "Emerging Entrepreneurs," "Sustaining Associates" and "Systematic Professionals."

An oxymoron is a figure of speech that combines two normally contradictory terms – like military intelligence.

Paradoxy-Moron describes those disruptively innovative inventors who encounter a paradox, and say, "Cool, what's the underlying phenomenon I can exploit?" They're drawn to the challenge of ushering in a disruptively new innovation and find funding or employment in locations near higher quality of life communities and premier destination resorts. We call them the "Breakpoint Inventors." They develop and champion radically new science, innovation, technologies or business models. These loosely connected ventures attract commercial innovators, R&D experimenters, and thought leaders. This is the type of organization that draws the following Myers Briggs Type Indicators: ENTP, INFJ, ISTP and INTJ.

Emerging Entrepreneurs in early to growth stages can't afford to staff up with more bodies. They recruit experts to eliminate the extra financial burden of benefits, but they guard their organization's core competencies while quickly managing increasing degrees of complexity. Marketing athletes, operational accelerators, resilient project teams, and core business groups develop the tools and manage the process of multiple new product introductions. They have to optimize the availability of internal and external team members – rolling people on and off projects -- as the critical path for each product dictates. You'll flourish in this type of organizational culture if you are an ESTP, ENTJ, ESFP or an ISFP.

Loyal survivalists anchor the **Sustaining Associates** culture. They manage people, technologies, processes, and organizational structures to sustain the innovation they've already mastered. Employees identify with the organization and have high affiliation needs that favor slower paced industries and cultures. These cultures become populated with internal change agents, analytical specialists and agile tiger teams made up of ENFPs, ISTJs, ENFJs and INFPs.

Finally, **Systematic Professionals** -- the experts who love their profession and their local location who find occupational homes in university research centers, professional practices, academic institutions and in standards-setting associations. Their identity is tied to their profession. Systematic Professionals by the very nature of their work make the best candidates for developing a "Mobile KnowCo" – a business based on selling knowledge in the form of books, reports, DVDs and other knowledge packages sold over the Internet -- that allows them to live and work anywhere in the world. But, many stay in one place – in or around university towns or urban and suburban centers where they find clients for their services. If you are an INTP, an ESFJ, an ISFJ or an ESTJ then these organizations represent your best fit.

7. Rehearse the future: play out the original plan or decision you want to make.

The trends that converge to influence economic cycles may not be easy to predict. But, by spinning four stories about the future, there's a much higher probability that a story thread in one or more scenarios will have alerted you to disruptions you would have overlooked. You will have given some thought to what you should do to adapt ahead of time. On the flipside of threats, hidden opportunities you haven't thought of before might fuel your progress towards your goals and dreams in new and more rewarding ways.

Here's what I discovered when I ran my plans through the stories I described:

Targeting growth industries is the best way to increase your career appreciation. Choose organizations in line with emerging consumer trends to build your marketability. Learn how to use newer technologies.

A new phenomenon is emerging thanks to "Web 2.0" technologies. You can make money while you sleep by packaging your knowledge and using the Internet to your advantage.

While we are in for a long downturn, new real estate opportunities will open up for savvy investors on the outskirts of premier resort communities.

The four talent cultures not only describe types of organizations, but they also describe the types of people who thrive then leave the organization as it grows through start-up, growth, maturity, decline, and reinvention.

I thrive in Paradoxy-Moron organizations and Systematic Professional cultures as well as in start-up to growth and reinvention phases. Your mileage will vary.

Start with your passions. Assess your personality. Focus on what you love doing. But don't stop there. Become a strategic career investor by following these seven steps to give yourself and your loved ones more choices and options. In the process, avoid a prolonged downturn while prospering with a better quality of life anywhere in the world you want.

Straight A's Ain't the Answer

John Hall

12

My brother Bob Hall graduated from Ohio State University's pharmacy school, a five-year program, in six years. He graduated with a 2.1 GPA out of a possible 4.0. While at Ohio State, Bob tried two different majors, engineering and veterinary medicine, before deciding on pharmacy. While in pharmacy school he waited tables in the university's Faculty Club and worked in our uncle's supermarket. He joined and was active in the Student Pharmacy Council and was elected president in his senior year. That same year he traveled from Columbus, Ohio to Las Vegas, Nevada to represent Ohio State's Student Pharmacy Council in the national pharmacy professional association.

After graduation, Bob went to work for a small pharmacy in upstate New York and was fired about six months later for telling the owner how he might improve his business. The pharmacy owner's final words to Bob were, "If you think you can do better, go out and start your own business." So he did. Bob talked McKesson and Robbins, the large pharmaceutical company, into funding him to open an ethical pharmacy, a pharmacy specializing in prescription drugs, over-the-counter medications, and medical durable goods. He then expanded into remodeling homes and cars for paraplegic patients and developing toys for paraplegic children, which he imported from England. He turned that business into a small chain of stores in Rochester, New York, and in 1984 was named Rochester's Small Businessman of the Year. A few years later Bob was invited back to Ohio State University, where he was recognized as one of the Pharmacy School's most outstanding graduates. He could not have gotten into their graduate school with his 2.1 GPA!

My brother's story illustrates several points about careers and success. First, there is no correlation between success in business and GPA in college. The summa cum laude graduate is no more or less likely to succeed in business than the C minus graduate. Second, we often the enter college with no idea what we want to do with our lives because we have so little life experience, and so like Bob, over two-thirds of us change majors at least once and up to thirty percent two or more times. Finally, of much greater importance to success in business is what is often called the soft skills: how you get along with others, your motivational level, and your willingness to take risks. In reality, the highly structured world of colleges and universities discourages risk-taking because academic achievement depends on following a very structured process with little room for experimentation. Intuitively, Bob Hall understood the value of the soft skills, such as getting along with others, and communication skills, and he was willing to take risks.

Top Tier Schools May Not Be the Ticket to the Boardroom
My brother Bob is typical of a number of high achievers:
- Half of all CEO's of Fortune 500 companies were average students in college.
- Most US Senators were C students in college.
- Half of US Presidents were C students in college.

- John McCain graduated in the bottom five of his class at the Naval Academy.
- General Colin Powell, former Chairman of the Joint Chiefs of Staff and Secretary of State, graduated from the City College of New York with a C average.
- Abraham Lincoln did not finish grade school.
- Harry Truman did not go to college.
- Most millionaire entrepreneurs did not finish college.

Over the 20 years I have been working as a career coach with management, executives, and technically educated men and women, I have seen little correlation between GPA and business achievement, even among clients who graduated from top-tier schools like Harvard, Wharton, or Stanford. This flies in the face of the commonly held assumption that graduation from a top-tier university is the key to business success. There is scant evidence that this is true. For example, a survey by executive recruiter Spencer Stuart finds that only 10 percent of CEOs currently heading the top 500 companies received undergraduate degrees from Ivy League schools. In fact more Fortune 500 CEOs received their undergraduate degrees from the University of Wisconsin than from Harvard, the most represented top tier school.

Unless you have been living in a wilderness cave, you are familiar with the fact that some of the movers and shakers in business today were college dropouts: Steve Jobs, the founder of Apple Computer, dropped out of college in his second semester; Bill Gates, the founder of Microsoft, dropped out of Harvard University at 19; Michael Dell dropped out of college and revolutionized computer marketing and sales. Several years ago I had a client who was president and CEO of a company worth $500 million who had dropped out of college at the end of his second year. I worked with a Harvard MBA who had plateaued at middle level management 15 years into his career.

There are truckloads of academic publications which document the relationship between GPA, IQ, and SAT scores and academic success in both undergraduate and graduate level study. However, there is very little research on success in business following graduation from college. What little there is strongly suggests that there is minimal correlation between GPA and business success.

MBAs and Business Success

For men and women planning a business career, an MBA has been considered the gold standard for a successful business career, "a union card for yuppies" as one observer put it. However, there is little evidence to support the value of an MBA as the key to business success. A 2002 study by two Stanford University professors, Jeffrey Pfeiffer and Christina Fong, found almost no correlation between an MBA, even from a top-tier school, and long-term business success. In the opening paragraph of their study titled, *The End of Business Schools? Less Success Than Meets the Eye,* they write, "What data there are suggest that business schools are not very effective. Neither possessing an MBA degree nor grades earned in courses correlate with career success. And there is little evidence that business school research is influential on management practice, calling into question the professional relevance of management scholarship."

Here is an intriguing suggestion from the book *Snapshots from Hell* by Peter Robinson, a respected tenured Stanford University professor. He suggests dividing the incoming MBA class into two cohorts. Have one section go through the normal MBA program, and the other do nothing except drink beer and play golf. Then compare the two groups after five to ten years in corporate life. The latter group, he bets will be far more successful than the first one. A fascinating suggestion, but I am betting that Stanford University is unlikely to test Professor Robinson's hypothesis.

College is important.

While the great majority of studies show little or no correlation between GPA and business success, they do demonstrate that a college degree increases the overall probably of business and/or career success when measured by lifetime earnings, whether one graduates summa cum laude or with a C minus GPA.

If GPA and top tier universities are not valid predictors of business success, what is? Research over the last ten years demonstrates that it is the soft skills or Emotional Intelligence (EI) as it has been labeled in recent years, not the academic stuff we learn in a formal university education. Daniel Goleman and other researchers have clearly demonstrated that emotional intelligence is a dramatically more reliable predictor of business success than either IQ or GPA. Dale Carnegie in his superb book, *How to Win Friends and Influence People*, published in 1936, wrote that success was based 15% on intelligence and education and 85% on how well we get along with our fellow workers. This is exactly the correlation that Daniel Goleman and others found in their research on emotional intelligence over 50 years later!

Adele Scheele, PhD, wrote *Skills for Success*, published in 1978. In the book she lays out why it is more important, while in college, to focus on what she called "real-world skills" rather than a high GPA. She writes, "Participating in the school play or on the debate team or running for political office, even if one loses, are more important in the real-world than the ability to get straight A's." Scheele goes on to write, "In short, the act of participating in a school play or a debate is more analogous to life than being a good student can ever be. The same kinds of learning and skills, both social and technical, are as important in business and professional life as they are in drama clubs, debate teams, 4-H projects, scouting, or any other extracurricular activity." Getting involved in these activities Scheele adds, "develops our ability to negotiate, organize, delegate responsibility, motivate others, and, in short, to lead."

So what does all the above really mean? It certainly does not mean don't go to college. It strongly suggests that if you're in college, make sure that you learn real-world skills by getting involved in activities that strengthen communication skills, negotiation skills, and leadership skills, even if it means achieving less than a 4.0 GPA. If you graduated years ago with a modest GPA, don't despair. All the evidence clearly shows that you can be just as successful, or as big a flop, as a 4.0 Harvard grad. The bottom line is to get out there and get involved in those activities that can increase your real world skills. Volunteer for community projects, join your professional association, speak, and write. Bottom line: you can be an average student from an average college and still become a business success. However, it is unlikely that success will come to those who don't have a high "GPA" in the soft skills of Emotional Intelligence.

Do You Need a Check Up? 13

Janet L. Newcomb & Michael D. Hardesty

Wondering what to do next? In a hurry to move forward? The last thing you may want to hear is, "Slow down!" But the truth is, "Go slow to go fast" is a phrase that has a great deal of merit.

As a culture, we are an impatient group with a bias for action. We want what we want and we want it now. Have you ever noticed that managers never seem to have time to thoroughly investigate a problem, understand its causes or develop appropriate strategies for its solution? The mantra seems to be, "Just fix it!" Then, later, it has to be done over because the fix didn't work – or even made things worse! Time is wasted that could have been productively applied to an accurate assessment exercise and strategic planning process, saving much time, agony, and money in the long run.

Careers can be the same. How many of us actually spend time figuring out what we need to do to have a successful career and develop strategies designed to move us in the right direction? The truth is that most of us usually spend more time planning our vacations than our careers.

As experts in organizational assessment, we have come to realize that our approach to helping companies become more successful can be applied just as effectively to an individual's life and career. There are three main areas of focus: the people stuff, the financial stuff and the operational stuff.

The People Stuff

It all starts (and ends) with people. It's important to have strong company leadership that creates and articulates a clear and consistent vision. Just as critical is the leader's ability to understand his/her strengths and weaknesses and choose the right people, placing them in the right jobs. The assessments we use look at such things as leadership competencies, company culture, employee engagement, succession plans, leadership development and employee training plans, communication and conflict resolution processes, reward and recognition systems, marketing and public relations plans and customer satisfaction.

This evaluation can be compared to your task when considering an individual career assessment. Here are some things to think about:

- How satisfied are you? Why or why not?
- Does your job match your values and further your long-term goals?
- Does it leverage your natural strengths?
- What things have you done that you most enjoy?
- What tasks have you always disliked?
- What might you like better and how will you know?
- Do you make a difference in your company and does that matter to you?
- Are you satisfied with your pay and benefits?
- Can your current job be reframed in a way that takes better advantage of your skills and experience?
- If not, do you need to be in another kind of job or a different kind of company or perhaps even a different industry altogether?
- Are you willing to relocate?

- How many more years do you want to work?
- Do you require additional education or training?
- Do you have an up to date resume and network of connections that market you effectively?
- Does your job leave enough time for family and/or other activities important to you?

The Financial Stuff

There are a number of financial processes that are important to a business. Tax returns, while important, may be the worst of all financial statements for running a company. You only have one year. They often contain both cash and non-cash items (i.e. depreciation), so they can have you more confused than ever about whether you're really making money.

Monthly financial statements are better. The balance sheet tells you whether or not the business is solvent, if the business is sufficiently liquid, what the assets consist of and who has a claim on those assets. The income statement shows you whether your company was profitable over a given period of time. However, the income statement is an abstraction that tracks only the promise and agreement of the company's transactions. It's not about cash. It does not show you how much cash you actually have on hand to spend.

A positive bottom line on your income statement is surely a good thing. On the other hand, profitability on the bottom line is no guarantee of success or even survival. Every year, thousands of businesses fail because they didn't have enough cash to stay alive. They "grew broke." You can operate a long time without profit, but you can't survive one day without cash.

Thinking about your career, cash flow is also the most critical item because it supports your freedom to make the career choices you desire. Don't become a slave to your job.

Work toward financial freedom by seriously considering the following:

- What are your income and expenses now?
- Can you reduce costs?
- Is there positive cash flow or are you tapping credit/savings on a regular basis?
- Is the trend up or down and why?
- What is the current trend likely to lead to and how soon?
- Are there future expenditures that can be identified and planned for?
- Do you have financial advisors you can trust?
- Will you have enough to achieve your goals, including retirement?
- In addition to current income, are you making wise investments for your future?
- Are there additional sources of income that can be readily developed?

The Operational Stuff

Without systems to run their businesses, owners really don't own a viable business. They own a job. Without systems the owner is not really building an asset to sell because no investor wants to buy a job. Because of changing market conditions, increased competition, and the lack of systematic processes, methodologies that allowed a business to succeed previously will not be good enough to sustain it at its current level long term, much less take it to the next level.

As sure as the sun will rise tomorrow, change will happen in business. The only question is, "Will a business owner proactively choose to embrace change or will they be forced to change by external circumstances?"

Jack Welch, the former CEO of General Electric said, "When the change outside your business is greater than the change inside your business, the end is in sight."

How about you – do you have just a job or are you putting processes in place to build a career? A few systems that have proved successful for many are:

- Contact management system to support effective networking
- Board of Advisors – a diverse group of trusted folks that will keep you on your toes and give you objective feedback
- Continuing education system
  - o Monitoring trends through reading and networking
  - o Keeping skills current through new experience and training

No matter how good you are at anything, the world is changing and you must remain marketable. In fact, the better you are at anything, sometimes the harder it is to change. Innovation and imagination are required to remain relevant in the 21st century career market. Will you proactively choose to embrace change or will you be forced to change? It's your choice. But as sure as the sun will rise tomorrow, change will happen.

"Choose a job you love, and you will never have to work a day in your life."

Confucius
551-479 BC
Chinese Philosopher

The Middle-Class Career At Mid-Life

14

John Hall

*B*lessed is he who has found his work; let him ask no other blessedness." This quote from Thomas Carlyle exemplifies middle-class Americans because we define ourselves first and foremost by our work. And though many of us say we would like to spend fewer hours pushing a pencil, attending meetings, and pounding away on a computer, and more hours with our families or playing with our boats and cars, it would be cruel punishment to take work away from us. For most of us in the middle-class, work is the single most important thing in our lives. Yet one of the great paradoxes of human development is that we are required to make the most important decision of our life as pimple faced adolescents or very young adults, before we have the knowledge, judgment and self understanding to choose wisely. Yet, if we put off the choice until we feel truly ready, that delay could produce even greater cost.

Choosing a Career

Many working class men and women stumble into the job market, unconcerned about preparation because they may consider it irrelevant to success in life. On the other hand, middle-class men and women are likely to plan their careers very carefully and persist in acquiring the necessary education and preparation, even in the face of economic hardship. In general, the higher the social and economic status of the family the more an individual is likely to plan a career, or at least the general outlines of one.

Middle-class adolescent men and women are under a lot of pressure when choosing a career because entry into the work world is becoming increasingly difficult. This is partly because there has been an overwhelming increase in the number of occupations from which to choose and because the increasingly complex nature of many jobs has made training longer and more expensive.

Motivations for choosing a given career can vary greatly. Individuals who choose business as a career usually make a rational appraisal of what is most important to them, which may be business' perceived power and income potential. On the other hand, men and women who chose an academic profession appear to be more motivated by autonomy, the desire to do scholarly work, and intellectual status.

Once the career path has been chosen, young middle-class individuals spend years as students, having to confine and discipline themselves to succeed in the educational process. Then after graduation from college they may spend two to four years in graduate school. After college, they may spend years in entry level work in engineering, sales, or management. Even hourly workers need years to explore, train, and move beyond apprentice, working their way into a union. All of this means that by the time individuals are really into their careers, beginning to advance and develop, they are in their late twenties or early thirties.

Career Structure and Stages

The career structure that most middle-class Americans visualize is of systematic movement up a status hierarchy, from a bottom position at the time of entry to a higher position after a certain number of years. Basically there are three career structures that middle-class individuals advance through until they reach the top of their professions, or as is more likely, plateau at mid-life:

- **Additive model:** In this model the worker spends a given number of years at each step in order to qualify for a promotion to the next step, as in the military service or the civil service.
- **Cognitive transformation:** In this model a certain amount of transformation in cognitive structure is expected to take place. The entry level MBA is supposed to gain in expertise and wisdom as he or she gains experience, thus becoming a different kind of manager or executive before moving up to the next step.
- **Personal transformation:** The focus here is more likely to be internal rather than external. It involves stages or sequences instead of rungs on a defined career ladder. Artists or writers experience this kind of career development. Progress is measured not by how many pictures or books are produced, but qualitatively, by the improvement in the pictures or books as one follows the other.

Career expert Judith Bardwick (1987) refers to three stages in a typical middle-class job. With each job the worker advances through in their career they will experience these stages until plateauing, remaining in stage three indefinitely.

- **Socialization**: In this stage people learn the parameters of work, what they need to do and whom they have to know.
- **Innovation**: In this stage there is a gain in confidence and the individual ultimately feels free of anxiety and uncertainty. Here one is most likely to reach true

achievement. This stage takes place between the sixth month and the third year.

- **Adaptation**: After being in a job between three to five years the work ultimately becomes routine. The worker may become indifferent toward the work and in time begin to feel powerless.

From Too Few to Too Many

From after World War II to 1975 everything favored the educated and ambitious individual. All the country's institutions, including government, more than doubled in size. Because the birthrate was the lowest in our history during the depression and relatively few went to college, the major problem for organizations was finding qualified individuals to fill management and executive positions. In this environment, ambition, ability, and hard work lead to promotion. Individuals stopped getting promotions only when they reached their level of incompetence. This was the now famous Peter Principle (Peter, 1969) in action. The basic tenant of The Peter Principle being, "Given enough time; and assuming the existence of enough ranks in the hierarchy; each employee rises to, and remains at, his or her level of incompetence."

In today's world of downsizing, lean and mean management, mergers and acquisitions, middle class jobs being moved to China, India, and who knows where else in the world, the competition for a middle class income is becoming much more intense. This abundance of educated, talented men and women competing worldwide will mean that many will not advance to even their level of incompetence, but will in fact plateau well below it. In effect, in today's global economy the Peter Principle is dead.

Career Plateauing

Career plateauing expert Judith Bardwick refers to the

"Rule of 99 Percent," which states: "In every large and complex organization, the number of positions at the highest decision-making level is always less than 1 percent of the number of employees." This means that long before retirement, promotions will end for almost all workers. Bardwick goes on to report that in today's well educated, over supplied work environment, only 10 percent of all middle-class workers will ever reach any level of even middle management. As a result many now in their thirties, educated, ambitious, disciplined, and qualified are facing the fact that they have plateaued. This plateauing occurs well below their potential ceiling with perhaps another 30 years of working life ahead.

Three Kinds of Plateauing

Plateauing is not a gradual process but tends to happen suddenly. At the beginning of their careers the middle-class individuals may get promoted every 18 to 24 months. Then at some point they realize that they have not been promoted in the last five years and are probably are not going any further. This is because the shape of the typical organizational pyramid is not the regular geometric form we usually envision but is very irregular, somewhat like markedly smaller rectangles piled on each other. Though interrelated, Judith Bardwick defines three distinct kinds of plateauing:

- **Structural**: Structural plateauing is marked by the end of promotions and is caused by the organization's structure. Structural plateauing will generate enormous problems for middle-class individuals for the next twenty years because of the oversupply of college educated men and women.
- **Content**: In content plateauing, the worker has become expert, knows the job completely and has little more to learn about it. This can lead to profound boredom. While structural plateauing is inescapable, content

plateauing is not. Lateral moves can give workers new content and thus reduce boredom.

- **Life**: When promotions end, some men and women develop a terrible sense of failure. Life plateauing is more profound, more total, and more serious than either content or structural plateauing. Those who are life plateaued feel a real sense of despair.

Quiet Desperation

It isn't unusual for a man or woman, as they move into middle age, to find the range of opportunities narrowing and ambitions becoming thwarted while still years from retirement. Today in most industries this plateauing begins at 42, and is trending downward. The first hint of plateauing may be exclusion from a company trip to another facility for training on new methods and technologies. Then a Catch-22 is set up where they are denied promotion because they lack the skills to do the job.

Since the middle-class man or women often derives their sense of worth from their career, they almost reflexively work even harder. They resist facing the fact that their career has flattened, even when it's clear to co-workers. When they finally realize that their career has stopped its linear advancement, middle-aged workers feel a marked sense of failure. There is no graceful way of backing down the ladder and taking a less stressful job. In fact, unless the worker has a disability, lateral movement is seen as almost un-American.

Classical Organization Theory and New Policies

Much of the disillusionment that the middle-age individual faces in their career may be related to Classical Organization Theory (COT). The basic principles of COT are that work should be divided into specialized tasks and that clear lines of authority should be established. Business relations should be kept impersonal and rewards should focus on rational economic issues. Some employees, usually those characterized by low self-esteem, prefer the structure of such organizations. However, most studies suggest that this management style leads to dissatisfaction, apathy, frustration, and mental health problems. Many studies of management level employees consistently show that they want self-direction and self-actualization in addition to income.

The technically trained and skilled individual can fall victim to a kind of promotion trap. For example, in many companies it is accepted practice to promote the most skilled engineer to a managerial position. However, few engineers have any management training and are expected to learn these skills once in their new position. The result is often an excellent engineer who becomes a poor engineering manager. They then become plateaued in a job they do not enjoy, do not do well, and thus may become a candidate for outplacement. Examples similar to this can be found in the educational sector when excellent teachers are promoted to administration. Quite often these excellent teachers become unhappy and as a result are poor administrators.

For the last twenty years the trend in the nation's management policies has resulted in middle class executive, management, and professional level individuals falling victim to mergers, company buy-outs, and company reorganizations. This trend has been compounded by the collapse of the mortgage banking industry. Nationwide tens of thousands of management and professional men and women are unemployed. Even when the industry recovers it is likely that half will need to look for another industry and some may need to completely change careers. Sociologist Kathren Bateson, interviewed on Bill Moyers, was speaking of this trend when she said, "The same kind of thing happens to foreclosed farmers who lose their farms and executives when their company gets bought out, and as it is said, restructured. They're both out on the street thinking, 'What do I do next?'

This is the century of the refugee. We live longer, both men and women. We have more potential discontinuities in our lives so that the creative life is likely to involve adapting and re-adapting maybe several times."

Attitude and Plateauing

Studies on Emotional Intelligence (EI) focus on a sort of chicken or an egg issue: "Does plateauing cause negative attitudes or are people with negative attitudes more likely to become plateaued than those with positive attitudes?" These studies suggest that men and women with high levels of EQ that have not yet plateaued continue to plan to advance in their careers by increasing their level of motivation. They are more likely to set goals and initiate steps to make things happen in their organizations. The plateaued worker, however, is more likely to interact with more people outside work, network less with fellow employees, and work fewer extended hours.

The Conflicting Emotions of Mid-Life

In his now classic study Levinson (1978) describes the conflicting emotions of many middle-aged men. They started to build what they hoped would be a stable, enduring life structure early in their lives. But, as they approach mid-life, some begin to feel constrained and to question the structure that just a few years before they had committed their lives to. The paradox is now that after he and his family have invested so much time, effort, and money, he finds this structure increasingly oppressive and feels compelled to break out. Yet to change is to tear the fabric of his life, to destroy much that he has built over the last ten or fifteen years. He feels overwhelmed by negative prospects: Staying is a kind of living death; breaking out may be destructive to loved ones and may not bring the better life he craves. In his struggle to work through these conflicting emotions he is likely to be moody, uncommunicative, and alternately resentful of others and blaming himself.

The Class Dollars Fell On

Many individuals don't feel successful until they feel in their soul they have reached the very top of the pyramid. A research project with Harvard Business school graduates of the class of 1949 is a vivid example of this need to be number one. As a group this class was so successful they were named by Fortune Magazine "The Class Dollars Fell On." The class included executive officers of Xerox, Elizabeth Arden, Johnson & Johnson, and other Fortune 500 companies. Most of the men in this class accepted the belief that unless they became number one, they had not quite made the grade. At the time of the study they were 53 years old. The central finding of the study was: the happiest were presidents the unhappiest were vice-presidents.

Despite the fact that everyone in the Class of 1949 had done exceptionally well in comparison to any other group of American men of their vintage, those who had not quite made it to the top seemed to be soured on life. They suffered from a vivid sense of being only number two. The sense of having fallen short stained most other aspects of their lives, their marriages, their relationships, and their health. Deprivation in love, sex, and health did not cause them nearly the same distress as that which stemmed from the feeling of being second-rate in their careers.

The Harvard Business Class of 1949 illustrates the value we put on successfully climbing the career ladder. But the American corporate system sets most of us up for failure because the entire structure is built on a pyramid. For every manager who makes it to the top, there are fifteen to twenty who will rise no higher than middle management. Most who embark on a corporate business career will never chair a meeting in the boardroom. Most military officers will not become generals, most musicians will never solo with a major orchestra, most writers will never make the best seller list, most artists will never have a picture exhibited in a major museum, and most of us fall short of our youthful dreams.

The Bored Manager May Be a Myth

Not all studies in this area are somber in their outlook. One study (Near, 1985) suggests that much of the above is myth. Near argues that the success of most organizations is due to the efforts of their Solid Citizens, their plateaued managers. According to Near, most plateaued managers are not bored but remain vital and productive. However, Near recognizes that her study is limited by its use of self-report, and suggests that further study in this area would be useful.

Burn Out

For many men and women, the feeling of being stuck and the resulting boredom leads to what has been termed job burnout. Burnout is a "disengagement or detachment on the part of a professional from any emotional feelings for the people he or she is serving in response to stress and overload." Or it may simply be due to a complete loss of motivation due to feelings of powerlessness. These feelings cause a malaise that affects work, health, and relationships. Symptoms that most burnout experts agree on are:

- A feeling of being trapped and not able to take it any more
- A feeling that nothing makes any difference
- A feeling that things will never get any better
- A feeling of having nothing more to give to others
- An increase in sickness and psychosomatic ailments
- The use of crutches such as alcohol or drugs

It seems more than coincidental that the accelerating increase of plateaued workers is being paralleled by an accelerating increase of job burnout insurance claims. In the last five years, such claims have risen by 40 percent in those states providing compensation for stress on the job. One study of both public and private sector employees, reported in U. S. News & World Report, found that close to 45 percent of the 18 public and private sector employees they studied suffered from psychological burnout. The report went on to state that in the heyday of the smokestack industries, physical injury was the chief problem facing average workers. Now, according to work-stress expert Dr. Charles Busman, "The computer age is taking its toll in the form of psychological pressure and personal conflicts that stem from mental strain and boredom."

Some who make it to the top do not escape the effects of burnout. Perhaps it is because their grandiose expectations of what the top should be like don't materialize. An uncomfortable listlessness may overtake them. The payoff may not seem commensurate with either the dream or the effort spent to reach it. For these employees, their personality would have resulted in burnout no matter how far they climbed before plateauing. Author Oscar Wilde defined this dilemma well when he said, "In this world there are two tragedies. One is not getting what one wants, the other is getting it."

Psychologists say that the forties bring a turning point for many men and women. Nearly 75% of middle level managers between 45 and 50 become downward anchored in their occupational orientations. They become inclined to look back at how far they have come occupationally, rather than focusing on how far they might yet go. Many individuals find themselves so security-bound that they cling to a job that is driving them crazy. Mid-life finds them desperately holding on, hoping not to make a mistake, so that they can successfully reach retirement. Living perhaps as Thoreau suggested, lives of quiet desperation.

The "Noon of Life"

Carl Jung distinguished the first half of life from the second and placed the dividing period at around 40. He observed that a resurgence of individuation might begin then, the noon of life as he called it. Until the late thirties, said Jung, a person's life is rather one-sided, with many valuable aspects of the self suppressed. At mid-life a person can, through the process of individuation, begin to nourish a treasury of archetypal figures within the self. This treasury can give individuals a more valued place in life where they will grow and enrich life in ways hardly dreamed of in youth. At the noon of life we become less aggressive, less assertive, more sensual, and more passive than when we were young. As Thoreau put it, "The youth gets together his materials to build a bridge to the moon, or perchance a palace or temple on the earth, and at length, the middle-aged man concludes to build a woodshed with them." Some men and women who are still advancing in their careers begin turning down top job offers because they do not want to make the kinds of personal sacrifices that such positions demand. Offers of more money, challenge, responsibility, harder work, and greater prestige as rewards become less important than health, families, friendships, and free time.

Career Change

Countless middle-aged men and women are beginning to believe that a shift in their career would give them a new lease on life. The late Peter Drucker, considered by many as the father of modern management, wrote an article in a magazine of limited circulation and received seven hundred letters and hundreds of phone calls from all over the United States - from ministers, professors, military officers, school principals, accountants, engineers, middle managers, civil servants, and others. According to Drucker, the reasons for this outpouring of interest in second careers are easy to understand:

"Today's working life span, having increased sharply since 1900, is too long for all but a few who reach the top and preserve their zest. Still in his mental prime, the typical knowledge worker is bound to become dispirited as he approaches middle age because he has reached his limit of contribution and growth in his first career - and he knows it."

Drucker suggest that a career change can be more rewarding than the bottle, an affair with a younger woman, the psychoanalysis couch, or other common attempts to mask career frustration. For the first time individuals are beginning to feel that work should be personally satisfying.

Golden Traps

There are golden traps in the form of institutional obstacles that discourage middle aged individuals from a career change. Pension plans, seniority rules, and early-retirement programs discourage making any kind of change if one doesn't have to. Another obstacle to career growth and change is the fact that though 80 percent of employers offer some kind of support for continuing education, only 10 percent of eligible employees take advantage of it. Unfortunately, middle-aged individuals are the least likely to use such educational benefits. The distressing fact is that most dissatisfied middle-aged individuals avoid retraining programs or further college level education. Some are willing to accept job downgrading rather than to educate themselves for new jobs. The longer the gap between previous learning and new education, the more serious this problem becomes. A study by B. L. Neugarten at the University of Chicago states:

"Real security of employment must rest on the ability to move from one job to another and the training of the middle-aged in new skills has a vital role to play. A new outlook should pervade education and training. We should get away from the ritual of the long learning period with formalized qualifications. Facts will soon become outdated. We must reorientate our thinking towards acceptance of learning through life in a flexible pattern of work and study."

Erickson's Seventh Life Stage

Men and women who are interested in retraining and career change differ from those who are not in that they have higher achievement motivation and are more interested in the social psychological aspects of their work. They don't see their current position as fulfilling either need. In effect, these employees represent Erik Erikson's Seventh Life Stage (Erickson, 1950), "striving to avoid a sense of stagnation and personal impoverishment."

In middle age it would not be unusual to find a 45-year-old London educated attorney with a successful practice give it up to become involved in radical political action, as Mahatma Gandhi did when he left South Africa to help his native India in its struggle for freedom. At 42, Benjamin Franklin left a successful printing business to enter government. At 37, Paul Gauguin left his wife, five children and a successful career as a stockbroker, to pursue his dream of becoming an artist. These men represent just a few who in countless intellectual, emotional, moral, and ethical managerial and reparative ways, feel that the middle-aged can help in maintaining and developing the culture.

Summary and Conclusion

There are no easy answers to the issues and problems discussed in this article. Today's baby boom, usually a middle-age middle-class man or woman, is in a work environment markedly changed from previous generations. Yet their expectations and value systems often inspire them to go for the success our American culture values and their personal goals strive for. The current large worldwide surplus of educated and talented men and women is making it increasingly difficult for middle-class men and women to equal their parents' level of personal or material success.

By mid-life, middle-class individuals fall into several emerging career paths. Some find themselves less worried about extrinsic values, pay, fringe benefits, and status. They have changed their focus away from career and more toward personal life. They have become more concerned with intrinsic and internal values. One third are contented and happy with where they are and with what they have accomplished. The rest are not contented and perhaps have had to lower their expectations. Still others find themselves struggling to keep up, desperately hoping for a promotion that may never come, hating every moment but still trying to make it to the top. A few seek the challenge, stress and excitement involved in changing careers. With them in mind, I feel the following lines are an appropriate conclusion to this review of the career issues facing middle-class men and women at mid-life.

"Come, visit us and when dull work
Grows weary, line on line,
Revive our souls, and let us see
Life's water turned to wine."

"The best time to start thinking about your retirement is before the boss does."

Author Unknown

Leap but Don't Trade Your Dream for a Nightmare

15

Steve Howard

How many times have you said to yourself, "That's it, I'm outta here?" More people are acting on that impulse – whether triggered by a significant emotional event like 9/11 or a death of a spouse, or a divorce or a layoff – or even something as mundane as when that invitation to join AARP arrives in the mail. But where do they go and what do they do? How do they avoid doing what my former neighbor and his family did – return disappointed, because the new community didn't measure up to their dreams?

At the Knowledge Labs, we've discovered two broad types of people who follow their passions to new destinations – Wireless Resorters and High Country Eagles. Two other broad types choose to stay put for vastly different reasons – the Wealthy Influentials and the Permanent Temporaries. Wireless Resorters (WR) -- those who head for resort communities of second homes with seasonal recreational pursuits, find neighborhoods in Premier Resorts, Maturing Resorts, Resort Suburbs and Distant Exurbs. High Country Eagles (HCE) search for more pristine Rocky Mountain High

115

quality-of-life towns and build their new nests in neighborhoods like Satellite Cities, Small Town Burbs, the Rural Country, and with other off-the-grid Rustic Eagles.

Some WRs buy or build an exclusive cabin in the woods (Premier Resorts) and run their wired or wireless lifestyle business from their deck in a mini-forest overlooking a mountain lake where they dock their cabin cruiser. Some HCEs cash in their chips, their six-figure salaries, to escape the rat race in favor of a small rural town (Small Town Burbs) and open a country store or hardware emporium. And some HCEs do something in between – they buy a hobby farm (Rural Country that borders on Distant Exurbs). But, they all leave the hustle and congestion and smog to look for small towns on rural roads as the answer to these questions:

- Who have I become?
- Do I want to be remembered as the person I have been up to now?
- Is it too late to put more meaning in my life?
- What will my life add up to?

What do they do? Our WR, a sole proprietor, chose not to be dependent upon the local market for her growing income stream. Our HCE, the former investment executive, caters to the "Tim the Tool Man" crowd in a tiny rural town of 337 residents. As you might expect our HCE hobby farmer — loosely defined as anyone who farms on smaller parcels than traditional farmers but not for their sole stream of income – depends on the land they own to a lesser degree than our former investment executive, but to a higher degree than our WR. Like the town hardware store owner, they often bring little or no hands-on experience to their new avocation. Their business acumen and marketing skills from previous jobs, however, can turn their pastimes into gainful enterprises with a little luck.

All three left the city after 9/11. Now don't get me wrong. Not everyone leaves when they encounter the opportunity. When couples become empty nesters many stay to be home for elderly parents or for nearby children.

Our investment banker longed to become a country squire, however -- to retire, to tend to his horses, to take up skiing again -- when an alternate entrepreneurial dream seduced him. Some do it for the money. Others do it to change the world. He just wanted to re-engage and learn something new about himself. He wanted to know if he was capable of working for interest and meaning rather than for money. Did he have something more to offer the world? Could he slow down and still be happy? Those who knew him well wondered. He steadfastly maintained that he could kick his Type-A personality in favor of the laid-back Jed Clampett lifestyle. You know, before Jed discovered that bubbling crude, or Texas tea, on the back forty and packed up his family and moved to Beverly – Hills, that is. In a way, his story is Jed's in reverse.

He felt life was passing him by and he needed to change before it was too late. He bought a retail business that forced him to come face to face with everyday locals with whom he had very little in common but who were also his neighbors. It's not always what you expect.

Drive through some of this country's small towns and you see bed-and-breakfast converted farmhouses up for sale. You drop in for a cup of coffee and conversation around the antique potbelly stove and hear sad retirees who invested in a general store and tell you they've gone from working five days a week in the city to seven days a week in the country – something they never bargained for. They'll tell you the workforce can disappear overnight. Kids who want to work are hard to find. Many leave because they won't be able to afford homes in the towns where they grew up. You can't blame them.

Here in the West, they call it "Californication." The locals don't appreciate the influx of outsiders who buy up a lot of real estate. Maybe a house next to the store can be converted into an old time ice cream parlor. Or another house on the edge of town can be renovated into a corporate retreat. Or that cabin on the lake will command high-end vacation rental income. In any case, the town needs to approve your development plans to expand septic systems, review zoning restrictions or drought-stimulated water permits. It all takes time.

And you can easily lose $70,000 your first year in business as you put in 40 to 60 hours a week dreaming of the day when you can cut the number in half and focus more on what gives you the most satisfaction. Like every good entrepreneur, you need to adopt a faith-based approach to revenue, one that rewards "being good at your craft. Money should follow that. If truth and beauty prevail, then this thing will make money."

Or, if that country store doesn't add spice to your life you might consider growing lavender on a nine-acre hobby farm in San Diego County's rural Valley Center. Why lavender? You can extract the oil, which goes into the dozens of products that you can sell online and to customers who flock to the farm each spring. Hobby or lifestyle farms account for roughly one million farms and continue to grow by about 2% each year

Boomers and Gen-Xers seek a rural life because they love gardening. Others simply want a quieter, simpler lifestyle and that feeling of safety in the countryside after 9/11. They embrace the green, organic movement with their children, while more and more harvest grapes for wine. Annual sales can bring in about $200,000 to defray the costs of running the farm.

Tradeoffs? You have to live far away from town and deal with many inconveniences but you can find that special spot far enough away to feel like they're living in the country but still be fairly close to mid- and large-sized metropolitan areas of 50,000 people or more. A little bit HCE – Rural Country and a little bit WR – Distant Exurbs.

Where? In an exurb called Temecula for instance. You can buy five-acre parcels of vineyard land, where you can build a home and other structures, such as a hobby winery (Distant Exurb). And then there are those who love growing food to sell at farmers markets. They don't make much money from it, but they love the camaraderie of the markets and watching the fruits of their labor end up on others' kitchen tables (Rural Country).

If that sounds like a lot of work, and you don't want to get dirt under your fingernails, head for the high ground and the resorts in the mountains where you reach a narrow ridge below the summit. The big view is spectacular. You see slopes ablaze with color descending to a magnificent highland lake lit by golden sunlight. But would you give it all up for a slower pace?

You may not have to. Before moving to the mountains, our Wireless Resorter spent years as an advertising and marketing exec in New York City and co-owned a firm that worked with financial services clients. After 9/11 she moved to a safer place – out of the cross hairs and flight path of the terrorists. Now she runs a Mobile Knowco -- a Mobile Knowledge Company – made possible more recently by the flexibility of the Internet.

She runs her marketing firm from a 1,500-square-foot pine cabin – in less space than a country store and in less space than the barn on the hobby farm. She works out of a small living room with seven windows - the three in front of her desk overlook hills of pine, maple, and birch trees. Every day she lunches on the deck, where she germinates ideas. With no fixed overhead that comes with a retail business or the upkeep of a five-acre farm, her annual revenues are nearly $1 million.

She admits the revenue is less than what her previous firm grossed in the city, but she points out with a sly smile, with no employees and lower taxes, she's keeping more of what she makes. Her clients include banking institutions you'd recognize.

Hold on now. She's living on a mountain resort in a forest running a Mobile KnowCo. How does she service her financial clients? The freelance designers, writers, and marketers she works with are based in three metropolitan cities. They meet through conference calls. Each participant is charged for a regular long-distance call, and the bridge is free. The service allows as many as 96 lines on a call.

She flies to the city at least once a month and travels frequently to visit clients elsewhere. She conducts daily activities in business lounges worldwide like checking e-mail, working quietly without office distractions, and returning calls. If she's not conducting important client discussions, she can locate Wi-Fi spots to use her laptop and make calls at a Starbucks.

What was her biggest fear when she left her old life in the big city behind? Becoming isolated and irrelevant. But the opposite has happened. She discovered that her mountain resort gives her a certain brand essence. It can't all be spectacular views and crystal clean air to breathe, right? She can't get the DSL or cable service like she could in the city. Her solution? Purchase a commercial-grade satellite dish and hide it out of the way at her property's edge away from her windows, her distant neighbors or the road. And she had to investigate the best business package to guarantee reliable service in case the satellite link goes down. With no cell reception there, her portable phone is just for traveling.

So there you have it, three different lifestyle examples of chucking the rat race for a higher quality of life.

One working on his Type-A personality, looking for meaning who can afford to lose $70K catering to the locals –

winging it with a faith-based business plan -- faking it until you make it.

One on the edge between the rural country and a distant exurb who transfers her marketing expertise to a hobby farm and brings in $200K to defray a portion of costs.

Or another who planned ahead with a Mobile KnowCo before she moved to her resort in the mountains and earned just under $1 million.

If you're looking for a vacation or second home in a resort community, you can compare tradeoffs. Depending on your preferences and pocketbook, you may choose among neighborhoods in premier, maturing, suburban, or exurban resorts.

With the right knowledge products producing multiple streams of residual income, you can overcome the challenge of having to make it in local rural markets. The Knowledge Labs discovered practical ways run a "Mobile KnowCo" by setting up "Knowledge ATMs" so you can make money while you sleep from customers all over the world. As with the four wireless resort communities you can live four varieties of vacation lifestyles in communities ranging from satellite city neighborhoods to remote off-the-grid rustic retreats.

How do you want to live the rest of your life?

"No man can succeed in a line of endeavor which he does not like."

Napoleon Hill
1883-1970
Author of *Think and Grow Rich*

Square Pegs, Round Holes

Janet L. Newcomb and Joanna Maxwell

16

There are many lawyers who are square pegs in round holes. Some became attorneys because they believed in justice or wanted to help people. Others were under family pressure to enter the law. Many became lawyers because they got good grades in school and didn't want to study medicine. All are struggling to fit into a mainstream legal career.

Have you ever felt like these lawyers?

- *Jenny: "Is this all there is?"*
  Jenny is a trial lawyer and enjoys her work - up to a point. The cut and thrust of court work and the intellectual challenge are stimulating, but sometimes she wonders what happened to the Jenny who dreamed of becoming a journalist, maybe even a novelist. Somehow drafting briefs and client letters isn't quite the same....

- *Dan: "I feel like some part of me is slowly dying."*
  Dan is in his early thirties and has practiced insurance law with a large firm since graduation. He is unmotivated by his work and feels hopeless about

doing more of the same for the next 20 years. He chose law because it felt safe and offered a good lifestyle, but is still drawn to his teenage passions of bicycle racing and environmental protection.

- *Corey's Father: "What is wrong with him? Is he careless, stupid, or what?"*
  Corey's father runs a successful mid-sized practice and was looking forward to his son joining him on graduation. However, Corey's first six months at the firm have been a disaster. Corey assumed he would become a lawyer like his dad but he is not interested in small details and double-checking his work: his mind gravitates to the big picture, the strategic idea, the creative solution. He is a willing worker and a great communicator but the fine details escape him time after time, making his father worried about leaving Corey in charge of anything other than the office Christmas party.

- *Steve: "I feel like I have to hang up half my personality with my coat when I arrive at the office"*
  Life in a straitjacket. That's how it seems to Steve, who feels as if his creative, passionate other side has to be shut away if he is to be successful in the legal world. He produces good, competent work, but is starting to show classic symptoms of depression.

The Problem

Whatever their reason for entering the legal profession, for Jenny, Dan, Corey and Steve, daily life as a lawyer just doesn't suit their personalities. The result is a clear lack of engagement with their work.

The 2005 Gallup Employee Engagement Index Poll identified three types of employees:

- **Engaged** – these employees work with passion and feel a profound connection to their company. They drive innovation and move the organization forward.
- **Not engaged** – these employees are essentially checked out. They are sleepwalking through their workday, putting time – but not energy or passion – into their work.
- **Actively disengaged** – these employees aren't just unhappy at work; they're busy acting out their unhappiness. Every day, these workers undermine what their engaged co-workers accomplish.

Not surprisingly, Gallup found that organizational performance is very dependent on an engaged workforce. So it is not just disengaged lawyers who suffer – their colleagues, employers and clients also pay the price.

A career mismatch can lead to dissatisfaction with working life, exhaustion from the effort of shutting down chunks of personality, stress, depression, and other health problems including substance abuse. The impact on relationships with family and friends can also be severe. Employers experience low work performance and costly errors that lead to client dissatisfaction, less repeat business and fewer referrals. Over time, high staff turnover, replacement costs and impact on office morale can be significant.

What can be done?

It is important to identify mismatches and to do something about it. Individual square pegs will be much more satisfied once they have found their right fit. Employers will find that productivity and morale soar with a fully engaged workforce - and of course client satisfaction will also increase.

Based on our experience as career development experts, we have been aware for some time of the significance of lawyer disengagement. The legal profession as currently practiced is highly logical, analytical and procedural. For a naturally left-brained attorney, these requirements can be an excellent personality match. For the more right-brained person (who is often attracted to the legal field because of altruistic notions of justice and helping people) the day-to-day reality of mainstream legal practice can be disappointing and frustrating.

We believe an approach developed by Dr. Katherine Benziger can provide insight into what is actually going on with many dissatisfied attorneys. This approach also helps them find a better fit for their legal training in a way that respects their natural gifts and personal values.

The Benziger Thinking Styles Assessment (BTSA)

The Benziger Thinking Styles Assessment (BTSA) is an updated application of Dr. Carl Jung's work in personality types. While other instruments may give an accurate picture of a person's current competencies, the BTSA can also identify whether or not these are consistent with natural preferences, allowing for a much more accurate assessment of true type.

Especially useful is the BTSA's ability to measure falsification of type, Jung's term for anyone whose most developed or used skills were outside their greatest area of natural preference or giftedness. This is critical since Benziger's work suggests that over half the population may be falsifying type at work, at home, or both – and we have seen much evidence of this in our work with dissatisfied attorneys. Being able to identify falsification of type is often vital for clients addressing career and work/life balance issues and can be significant in understanding the relevant issues for disengaged attorneys.

Benziger's assessment identifies four primary modes of thinking:

Basal Left (BL): Basal Left thinking is ordered and procedural, distinguished by the ability to *repeat an action consistently and accurately over time.*

Basal Right (BR): Basal Right thinking is *spiritual, symbolic and feeling-based.*

Frontal Right (FR): Frontal Right thinking is *visual, spatial and nonverbal.*

Frontal Left (FL): Frontal Left thinking is *logical and mathematical,* excelling at precise *critical analysis and diagnostic problem solving.*

Preferences

According to Benziger, each of us has an in-born, neurologically based preference for one of these four modes of thinking. Although we can all develop competencies in any of the four modes, it will be easiest and most energy efficient to develop competencies in our preferred mode. It will be next easiest to develop competencies in the auxiliary modes adjacent to our preference. The most difficult area (our natural weakness), and one that usually comes late in life if at all, is the area diagonally opposite our natural preference.

What does all this mean for individuals? Try our thinking styles quiz to find out more about the characteristics of each type and to see what your preference might be. (For the most accurate information, including your degree of falsification of type, a complete BTSA assessment is necessary.)

Quiz: What is your thinking style preference?

There are six questions for each style. Your highest 'Yes' score is likely to be your strongest preference and your highest 'No' score to be your least preferred style.

BENZIGER BREAKTHROUGH MINI ASSESSMENT

Frontal Left	Frontal Right
1. Do you have well defined goals? 2. Can you calculate the most direct, efficient and cost-effective strategies for any situation? 3. Do you enjoy management positions in which you control key decisions? 4. Are you skilled at manipulating circumstances into alignment with your desired results? 5. Do you prefer technical, mechanical, or financial work? 6. Do you excel at the use of tools and/or machines? **Score out of 6:** Yes: No:	1. Do you tend to think in metaphors and concepts, expressed as internal pictures or movies? 2. Are you a master of integration, innovation and imagination? 3. Are you bored with routine? Do you seek stimulation, new concepts, new information, new adventures? 4. Do you store material in stacks or piles around your office (rather than filing it neatly away). 5. Do you have a quirky sense of humor? 6. Are you interested in humanity and ideas about its evolution and development? **Score out of 6:** Yes: No:
Basal Left	**Basal Right**
1. Do you derive a sense of accomplishment from following established routines and procedures? 2. Are you a master of detail? 3. Are you loyal, dependable and reliable? 4. Are you valued for the consistency of your work and the thoroughness with which you complete tasks? 5. Are you naturally conservative, with traditional values? 6. Do you prefer to approach tasks and solve problems in a step-by-step way? **Score out of 6:** Yes: No:	1. Do you pick up subtleties and shifts in others' moods and emotions? 2. Are you aware of nonverbal signals? 3. Do you instinctively reach out to others through words and gestures? 4. Would you describe yourself as naturally caring? Is how a person feels of utmost importance to you? 5. Do you value compassion, relationship and interpersonal harmony? 6. Do you motivate others to join in by sharing your excitement, enthusiasm and support? **Score out of 6:** Yes: No:

(c) 2008 - Dr. Katherine Benziger

Introversion and Extroversion

The other key factor of equal importance to the four thinking modes is level of introversion and extroversion. This determines the context in which a person is most effective - a highly extroverted Frontal Left will succeed in situations that a highly introverted Frontal Left would find most uncomfortable.

Approximately 70% of the population enjoys a balance of extroversion/introversion and thrives on moderate stimulation. Another 15% of the population requires highly stimulating environments, such as labor negotiations or active courtroom litigation, while the remaining 15% need lower levels of stimulation such as legal research to be comfortable and function effectively.

Understanding both the preferred thinking mode and where an attorney falls on the extroversion/introversion continuum is critical to successful job matching. An extroverted Frontal Right lawyer may be ideal for a busy in-house role where strategic advice to management is a big part of the job and there is a team of junior lawyers to handle drafting and fine detail work. The same lawyer would be extremely frustrated stuck in a back office reviewing detailed corporate merger agreements. Equally, to ask an introverted Basal Left to handle trial work (or any court appearance) is a recipe for disaster; though they may be ideally placed to document the underlying legal points back at the office.

Would you like to feel like this?

- *Georgia: "I'm using all of my training - and all of my talents."*

Georgia held a B.A. in Sociology and attended law school because of a strong interest in social justice and helping people. Although she enjoyed her studies, including writing for law review, she realized that the evidentiary and procedural (Basal Left) aspects of practicing law would be tedious and frustrating. Looking for a way to use her law degree and mediation training in a role more suited to her natural talents, she shifted her career from contract negotiator to corporate Ombudsman.

This was a perfect match for her extroverted, creative (Frontal Right) and people-oriented (Basal Right) personality. In addition, her analytical skills (Frontal Left) served her well in diagnosing cases likely to result in litigation if not resolved. She achieved litigation avoidance savings of $2,000,000 per year and thrived on the continual challenge of having new problems to solve.

- *Matthew: "I love my writing and have space to breathe."*

Matthew entered law because he was fascinated by legal concepts (Frontal Right/Frontal Left), but when he joined a large law firm on graduation he found the demands of casework and drafting overwhelming. As an introvert, he was challenged by the degree of client contact his job required, as well as the inevitable interpersonal elements (Basal Right) and distractions of life in a law firm. Some days he felt so hemmed in that he literally couldn't breathe properly.

Following some soul searching, he arranged some coaching sessions to explore his personality type and to understand why his current job was so unsatisfying. With the insights he gained into his strongly introverted Frontal Right/Frontal Left personality (and almost total lack of Basal Left strength) he started writing articles for a local newspaper commenting on the law from a broader perspective. After some time, he was offered a regular column and also started to sell his work to other publications across the country.

- *Ros: "Now I'm having some fun."*

Ros was in her mid-thirties and an associate with a boutique corporate law firm in a large city when she became pregnant with her first child. She felt unfulfilled in the law, as if part of her personality had no expression. Ros loved chatting (Basal Right) and was also clever and creative (Frontal Right), but struggled with the detailed drafting work her job entailed (Basal Left). She felt she didn't fit in the legal world and that this was reflected in her lack of career success.

She decided to use maternity leave as an opportunity to re-think her career and explore more creative and satisfying options. When her year away from the workforce was up, Ros had rediscovered her passion for creating elegant, exciting gatherings and was well on the way to starting a business arranging sophisticated social events.

Conclusions

Remember Dan, one of our initial case stories? After a number of sessions analyzing his personality type and the implications of this for his legal career, Dan realized that he actually did enjoy being a lawyer, but as an extroverted Frontal Right/Frontal Left he was quite unsuited to the fine detail and repetitive nature of life as an insurance attorney. He has now found a position with a regulator, investigating fraud by financial advisors and preparing prosecutions, a much better fit for him. (He still races his bicycle on weekends.)

Steve, on the other hand, has decided to abandon the law in favor of a career as an artist. Although he is just starting out, his depression has already disappeared and he is full of enthusiasm for his new life.

The ability to understand your own personality strengths (and challenges) can be the key factor in crafting your ideal career path. Sometimes, taking a long hard look at what really satisfies you can give you the courage to move into a new arena where you can shine, whether this necessitates leaving the practice of law or reshaping your career within the law. For one attorney, the answer may be to develop that longstanding dream of being an actor; for another, all that may be needed is a shift into teaching law or writing appellate briefs rather than business contracts.

Benefits for individuals include greater job satisfaction, better alignment of talents, less stress and anxiety and more all-round energy, life balance and happiness. (An added bonus is your employer's increased satisfaction with you!)

Benefits for employers include better use of human capital, greater productivity, improved morale and less disruption, less sick leave and stress leave (and less staff turnover) as well as greater client satisfaction.

Resources

Dr. Benziger's book *Thriving in Mind: The Art and Science of Using Your Whole Brain* is available from her website (www.benziger.org), along with other articles, resources and suggestions for further reading.

A New Kind of Diversity: Four Generations at Work

17

Rochelle Burgess and Hal Hendrix

We live in a fascinating, educational and energizing workplace culture in America. For the first time in history, we have four distinct age generations in the workplace at the same time. They each bring a different frame of reference and each presents unique challenges and opportunities for organization leaders. They each bring unique contributions to the workplace as well. While successful leaders have long recognized that hiring in their own image (i.e. a personality or business approach or even ethnicity similar to their own) is not the best strategy, diversity now includes yet another dimension! The BIG QUESTIONS relative to generational differences are:

1. How can leaders identify and capitalize on both the uniqueness and similarities between the generations?
2. How can leaders build and enhance effective working relationships between the generations?
3. What specific strategies, tools, and language can be used to create an organization of motivated, dedicated employees who will take the Company to the next level of success?

Our research over the last five years, and interviews with hundreds of employees in various industries, has provided us with an encouraging, sometimes humorous outlook.

A Comparison of the Generations:
Generation Y (age 18-31)

They are also known as the "Millennium Kids," the "Net Generation," and the "Re-boot" Generation. They are perceived by the other generations as very bright but slackers because they always appear to be text messaging. They want some structure in their jobs but have no respect for authority. They want empowerment, even though they are green in terms of business savvy, and want continuous feedback. Their unique contributions include their technical savvy; their high respect for those with wisdom, knowledge and experience; their thirst for business education and continual learning; their unyielding desire to challenge assumptions; their commitment to the goal at hand; and their great desire to contribute their creativity and make a difference in the company.

Because they have typically been raised in an environment where everyone is allowed to win and no one is allowed to lose, they enter the business world filled with self confidence but are afraid to make mistakes. To other generations, they require an unreasonable amount of continuous feedback and encouragement on their work progress.

Generation X (age 32-43)

They are also known as "Baby Busters" and the "NeXt" Generation. They are perceived by the other generations as great problem solvers but too independent, with disdain for consensus building. They are great strategic thinkers but lack good listening skills. They are very good at networking but have little patience with interpersonal skills. Their unique contributions include innovative strategic planning, networking, and partnering across organizations; critical thinking skills in re-assessing the goal; and their appreciation of the need for work/life balance. Because they have typically been raised in an environment where they learned early to take care of themselves and meet their own needs, they entered the business world filled with self confidence but moreover, an impatience for delays in decision making. To other generations, they may unreasonably lack team player skills and/or willingness.

Baby Boomers (age 44-62)

They are also known as the Boomer Generation and the Viet-Nam Generation. They are perceived by the other generations as great sources of experience and business savvy and good mentors but lacking an understanding of the need for work-life balance in the 20's, 30's and 40's (i.e. they tend to be seen as workaholics until approaching retirement themselves). They have good listening skills and are customer focused but still sometimes refuse to realize the extreme possibilities that using modern technology can offer. Their unique contributions include their ability to be role models for customer focus, teamwork, collaboration, and focusing on the goal at hand as well as long term goals. Because they were typically raised in an environment where it was important to give families and children material possessions, they entered the business world with a focus on attracting title, status, and toys that proved their success. They were also raised in an environment that was customer focused, both internal and external to the family. To other generations, they may appear too status conscious and too slow in decision making.

Mature Generation (age 63+)

They are also known as the Traditionalist Generation, the Silent Generation, and the GI Generation. They are perceived by the other generations as being good listeners but still convinced only by their own experience and answers. They are good business mentors but too command/control oriented. They are strong decision makers but not empowering enough to let others make the decisions. Their unique contributions include their business experience, wisdom from life experience, ability to mentor others, and commitment to the long term goal. Because they were typically raised in an environment where integrity, respect for authority and attention to hard work were demanded, they entered the business world with a need for clear structure, chain of command in decision making, and trust in agreements by handshake. To other generations, they may be perceived as stubborn and overly concerned with respect when it is not warranted.

The Challenge

There are valid reasons for the negative perceptions toward each generation by the others. There are also very logical and effective ways to approach the differences by embracing each group's unique contributions. Dissertation research and hundreds of personal interviews over the past few years have suggested some interesting recommendations. As we share these, audiences tell us our recommendations are innovative and useful!

We know that some things are age and maturity driven – the baby boomers were the rebels of their day who, in their twenties, wanted to do things differently and change the world – just as the Millennial Generation (Gen-Y) employees of today have the need to make a difference in the company they work for and have an impact on their world.

Some things are generational driven, however, based on the environmental experiences during the formative years. For example, Generation-X employees are typically problem solvers and strategic thinkers who don't like being told to work on teams. They are independent thinkers who have a disdain for forced consensus decision-making. However, they are outstanding at partnering with others throughout the organization to solve problems. This is because they were also typically latch-key children of single parent or working parent households where they were included in family discussions of budget planning and vacation planning. They were taught to be very independent in taking care of themselves, making decisions, and managing their choices. This is a much different environment from the typical Generation-Y employee, even though he or she may also have two working parents. The Generation-Y employee who is seen text-messaging at work is often calling a parent or mentor to discuss a current workplace decision.

Recommendations

Both leaders and peers within organizations can look at a number of approaches and actions that can be taken immediately to (a) understand the other generations' values and expectations in the workplace; (b) take advantage of the strengths and perspectives that each generation offers; (c) recognize the similarities and that a way of thinking, versus numerical age, is key to building a stronger values-based organization; and (d) gain a better appreciation of the generational diversity in the organization.

Generation Y

Generation Y employees tell us one of their biggest frustrations at work is not receiving enough feedback from their managers. They require continual feedback in order to be comfortable that they are making a difference and making progress (and not making mistakes). We have recommended to their managers (usually Generation X) that tasks and projects be assigned with a clearly expressed result in mind and an agreement for milestones to be reached along the way. The Gen-Y can be comfortable knowing that feedback will be received often, and the Gen-X manager can be comfortable that he or she won't be interrupted constantly with the question, "How am I doing?" The Gen-X leaders tell us they want their younger employees to spread their wings and experiment and do things over if necessary, the same way their own generation learned to be successful.

They want their employees to bring new, innovative ideas to the table. Their Gen-Y employees tell us, however, that while they are excited to do that, they see their gift as enhancing and building upon the contributions made by Generation X. They also fear that their contributions will not be considered good enough in the business environment so they need to know they are on the right track. Therefore a balance of feedback can be beneficial for both generations.

Generation X

What is our recommendation for Gen-X employees who don't want to be part of a team? Our incumbents have agreed that if we ask them to partner with anyone they need, or even specific individuals in various departments, to solve a company problem, and if we say that we want everyone involved to agree on the solution, they have no difficulty in meeting that requirement. We simply called it partnering instead of cross-functional teamwork! There are some nuances to each type of process, of course, but the outcome still has input and agreement from all the necessary stakeholders.

Baby Boomers

Generation X managers often perceive their Baby Boomer supervisors, peers and employees as not being quick enough to make decisions. A balance between focus on process, milestones and end results can address the needs of both generations by focusing on both the short tem and long term goal. If timeframes are in place for each of these elements, then the Baby Boomer's need for data, process, and input from others – i.e. decision making in a reasonable manner – can be balanced against the Gen-X's need for decision making in a timely manner.

Mature Generation

Other generations, while thankful for the knowledge and history that the Mature Generation members bring to the organization, are often frustrated by the older generation's insistence on what will or won't work, how things should be, and working through a specific chain of command. We have learned Mature Generation leaders and employees are more open to new, innovative ways of doing things if they have the ability to (a) contribute verbally up front the cautions to be anticipated, and (b) critique afterward what worked and didn't work and offer ways to improve upon the new ways. In this way, they become part of the solution, rather than perpetuators of the old ways and stuck in the same problems. They no longer see the old ways of doing things as the only alternatives and are more able to see new possibilities.

Additional Recommendations

We should also consider other personality style differences, styles of absorbing information, and methods of making decisions and approaching issues, such as the Myers-Briggs styles and the Visual/ Auditory/ Kinesthetic – and we have added Intuitive/Digital styles!

These personality and learning styles add value to the discussion of age diversity and demonstrate that employees may share very strong characteristics across generational lines which bond them in various scenarios regardless of their age. The similarities establish the connection or bond between individuals, so that the differences become the basis for conversation rather than conflict. Establishing commonalities is the key to appreciating differences as unique contributions in any situation.

References:

Lancaster, L.C. & Stillman, D.(2005) *When generations collide: Who they are. Why they clash. How to solve the generational puzzle at work*. New York: HarperCollins Publishers Inc.

Martin, C.A. & Tulgan, B. (2002). *Managing the generation mix: From collision to collaboration*. Amherst, MA: HRD Press, Inc.

Zemke, R., Raines, C., Filipczak, B. (2000). *Generations at work: Managing the clash of veterans, boomers, Xers and Nexters in your workplace*. New York: American Management Association.

Choosing not to be Miserable at Work

18

Steve Amos

Y ou spend massive amounts of time at work. Work gives you status. Your income comes from your work. Your income supports your family. And most of your problems come from work.

You work with demanding customers and coworkers of all cultures, political persuasions, and religions; see strange foods and irritating manners; and handle all types of bosses from smooth salesmen to irrational dictators.

Most people do not get fired from jobs for incompetence. They wear out their welcome with poor attendance, coming in late, leaving early, or maintaining the welcoming attitude of a large green ogre. This results in their fellow employees leaving them out of the daily give and take. Job performance follows attitude with missed deadlines, sloppy work, and others taking over your workload.

How We Get Miserable

First, remember when you got the job? You wanted it, begged for it and said, "Pick me, Pick me! I will do a good job." Think how thrilled you were to get your job. Were you ecstatic? You were proud. You told everyone about your new job and company.

Gradually the job lost its freshness. Problems arose from grumpy coworkers, complaining customers, and poor suppliers, causing most of us to accumulate a ton of bad attitudes. After a while, you start complaining about the alarm, the commute, the grind, the workload, his mess, her perfume, the weather (even though you work inside), politics, decisions, demanding customers, and the boss. What about work don't you complain about?

This puts you in the rut that leads to getting passed over for new assignments, raises and promotions. The downward spiral gets worse when others are getting ahead and you stay right where you are. Be honest, are you thrilled with your performance?

You can be happy at work.

Look for where you can make a difference. How can you make the customers happier? How can you help increase sales? What can you accomplish?

Fall in love with your profession again. Read business journals, magazines, and websites. Compare your products and services with competitors and see where you can improve. Brian Tracy points out that the difference between top performers and the average is top performers often give just 1% more effort, far less than you might think. Persistence, service and a little extra make all the difference.

Mentor your coworkers, especially newer employees. They will appreciate the help and you will feel unbelievable joy by helping them. You will not believe how much you learn by teaching. Helping others is what we are born to do.

Create business relationships. Respect the contributions of others and ignore their unimportant shortcomings. Let other people be right. Learn about your coworkers and find areas that you respect about them. The biggest donor to charities I worked with was a third shift machine operator who had adopted four kids. I would never have met him if I hadn't volunteered to help a charity drive. Take pride in where you work and who you work with.

Laugh a little when things don't go right. Humor often makes our daily trials livable. In this politically correct world, you can always make fun of yourself and others will love you for it.

You will be surprised in a few months by how much the right attitude results in more fun and productive work. Go enjoy your work and start looking forward to Mondays.

Wolfgang Christoph, Brian Tracy and Dr. Roberta Shaler deserve credit for the ideas presented in this article.

"If money is your hope for independence, you will never have it. The only real security that a man can have in this world is a reserve of knowledge, experience and ability."

Henry Ford
1863-1947
American Automobile Manufacturer

Unlearning What You Were Taught

19

Steve Amos

Do you know that much of what you have learned is wrong? It is not your fault. Schools teach basic knowledge, not the answers to the big questions in life. Schools want you to behave in class, pass tests and score well on standardized tests so you can go to college. They teach you to sit still, be quiet, and pay attention to your teacher.

College professors have their own agenda about what you should learn. College used to promote debate about different ideas and consider different viewpoints respectfully. Now it is more like "We know what is good for you" at most colleges.

Who taught you how to manage money? I learned nothing about finance until I started working and had to justify capital investments. Finance is a key life skill schools ignore.

Our parents and grandparents taught us what they knew about survival and getting by. Our parents could not teach us all the ways to thrive and excel because they were not taught how to thrive and excel. You have to learn that on your own.

Seriously look at the things you learned from adults as a kid. Were you taught these lessons as a kid?

- Study hard, get an education, and get a good job
- Do it the way you were taught
- Work hard to get ahead
- Improve your weaknesses
- Follow the rules
- Wait your turn
- Big business is evil
- You can't fight city hall

Unlearning Schooling

I have spent my life unlearning my schooling. I was taught to sit still and be quiet, wait my turn, don't ask for what I want, and be a good boy. These beliefs are not effective in the real world. Patience is good, but you must ask for what you need. You must act to get what you want, not sit quietly waiting for someone else.

Fortunately my family does not always follow these rules. Curiosity is encouraged. It is okay to be unique. It is okay to think differently. We are encouraged to think about solutions to problems. Mom's expression was, "Humor him (or her). They may be a genius." We were taught that it is good to work hard but have balance in your life. Work is not your only purpose for being. You have take time to give back.

In my twenties I realized that no one knows it all. My career was progressing as well as others. Why was I afraid to speak up? We all have knowledge to share. I learned from the lowest workers in the factory as well as from the bosses. Being fair, I was not doing too badly. I outgrew my shyness by unlearning it.

What You Can Do

So how do you learn about the big questions in life? What are my gifts? What is my calling? How can I best contribute? You don't learn these in school. I started hanging around successful and positive people. You will find that successful people think differently. You don't have to make every mistake yourself. Here are important things I learned after my formal education ended:

- Get your daily work done early. Some work is less pleasant than other work. It still has to be done and successful people get all their work done effectively. Get in the habit of doing things you are uncomfortable doing as soon as possible. Then they are out of the way.
- The best productivity technique is delegation. It is worth paying other people to do what they do better than you, so you can focus on your gifts. Do you do surgery by yourself? How about dentistry? Practice law? Spread the workload among your coworkers. There are jobs you give your boss to complete. It is his job. Let others cook, clean, keep books or do specialties which are not yours. Focus on your gifts.
- Budget time for special projects, training, researching business, reading industry articles, and business research after the work is done. Life is for learning, so keep learning every day.
- Nothing goes as planned. There are often several ways to do something. You have to create back up plans. You need to be flexible and resourceful. Many successful projects are the result of many revisions to the original idea.
- Do what you are passionate about. Share and teach what you learn.
- Consider becoming an entrepreneur. It is less risky than working for someone else. If you work for yourself you have some control over your life. Work hard and become a business owner or investor. If you don't desire to run your own business, find three of your best gifts to earn a living with.

- The soft skills of working are important. Meeting other businesspeople, making presentations, influencing others, creating ideas, making small talk, and selling your ideas are more important than expertise in business. It is not what you know that is important, it is how you make people feel.
- Make constant personal improvement your goal. Be 1% more effective or efficient every day and you will be closer to your potential every day. Practice focusing on one task at a time. See how quickly you can get it done. Then reward yourself and take on the next task. Can you imagine how much better you will be after only one year? The competition will not be able to keep up.
- Write down your dreams. No matter how wild, ridiculous, oversized, costly, or crazy, write them down. Take one dream, the one that excites you the most. Visualize yourself completing it. Feel how great it is to have done it. Visualize the rewards, the accolades, the pride of your friends and family. Now write down a few steps to make this happen. Break down the earliest steps into small actions. Do one of the simplest steps. Read an article, make a phone call, write something, take more notes, or just take one action. You are on your way to making a dream real. Start now!

Try some of these ideas today. See what works and don't expect to be perfect doing them the first time. Best of all, you just unlearned something you were taught.

Redefining Success

20

Steve Amos

In high school success was passing your courses and graduating, having friends, a date on Friday, and a date for the Prom.

In college success was still passing your courses but more important was figuring out your major. Most of us had no idea whether we would like the career we chose, but we chose it anyway.

After college, success was getting your first job and an apartment. Friends and good times were also a priority. The adventurous traveled. Most of us tried to figure out how to make our work meaningful.

The next success was finding a partner to love and who would love us and getting married.

Family comes after marriage. Success was buying a house or condo. As the family grew, success was getting a bigger house.

Getting promoted or getting a better job was our next criterion of success. Some chose to be self-employed instead.

At some point, the economy or business cycle changed and success was keeping our job as others were laid off.

Maybe your next success will be retiring. Perhaps you will consider it a success to find part-time work to keep you busy or play more games of golf.

While these are fine goals, I think most are not a good definition of success (with the exceptions of love and family). Here's a better definition of success.

Success is when we take care of people. Success at work is taking care of customers. Success is earning a living. Raising good children is a success. Taking care of your spouse is success. Success is anything we do to make the world a better place.

Success is when we do for others selflessly. Success is not about us, not what we own, but about serving others. We succeed when we help any way we can by giving either our time or money. Volunteer at charities or church. Volunteer in your schools or neighborhoods. Take action for others.

Isn't that a better definition of success for you to live by? Change your definition of success and you can leave a better world. Then you are really succeeding!

Crossing a Picket Line   21

Steve Amos

I n 1986 I went to work for a company on strike. Who in their right mind would cross a picket line? I had been unemployed for six months, and thought I had landed a job with one of my dream companies. It was the fifth interview for the third job opening there since I had been laid off. I was thrilled to get the job. Then the company went on strike on the same day I interviewed. Now what?!?

As a non-union manufacturing engineer, it did not make sense to me that anyone could strike for very long. I figured the strike would end in several weeks and it would take the company three weeks to process me to start work. My career had always dealt with management and production and I respected both groups of people. The strike should end soon.

Background

I assumed this knowing little of the history of the problems between management and the union. The situation was ridiculous. I've never seen two groups fight so hard to hurt each other. The union filed numerous false claims that the company was violating employment laws, government contracts, forging quality reports, and spilling milk. The company tried to catch the UAW intimidating employees, breaking laws, and being from outer space.

The UAW had plenty of savings and the financial support of other unions, making it easier for them to protest, picket, and intimidate. The UAW leaders were still getting their salary. However, the workers on the picket line were making less than a quarter of their previous salary and most lost cars, furniture, savings, and homes while striking. It was miserable.

The company still had government contracts to deliver. They transferred top management into production and hired replacement workers to make the products. They had reserved enough money to wait for a court decision that could be years away. That was their plan.

The company interviewed the willing, the unemployed, people off the streets, and hired 25 to 50 people per week. It was surprisingly easy to train new people to make better quality product than you would think. How hard is it to load parts and push a button on a machine? These people wanted to work and were grateful for their new jobs. Within three months contracts were back on schedule despite the strike and union members were shocked how easily they had been replaced.

Life during a Strike

Why should you never work for a striking company? It is not fun crossing a picket line. The strikers scream vulgarities, insults, and threaten your life for working. Basically everyone looks like an idiot. The police, unionized themselves, have the uncomfortable job of separating everyone. The police deserve respect for doing this tough job.

Other games go on in a strike, mostly intimidation. The union would recognize our cars or follow people home. Cars were vandalized, flowers trampled, and homes watched for the chance to commit more mayhem. I woke up more than one night and saw someone parked outside watching my house. I slept with a camera and a gun nearby. The camera to catch them in the act and the gun was for protection.

I went bowling one night and came out to find my car with four flat tires and coated with paint stripper. I had to get a ride home, borrow a friend's truck, and take half a day off to replace the tires. The company paid for the tires and a complete paint job as well. Eventually the union put sugar in my gas tank and that killed the car.

Effects of the Strike

The company's customer sales base included a lot of union members. Sales dropped as business went elsewhere or waited for the strike to end. The company lost sales and marketing opportunities during the years the strike lasted.

Then the company management started treating the replacement workers the way they treated the union workers. The employees were suspected of cheating. The company had to follow the contract but management kept the same attitude even with different workers. Is it any wonder the union relationships were strained before the strike?

The corporation lost the lawsuit after four years and cut its losses by selling the division to the union. The replacement workers all lost their jobs to the union members.

However, the long strike had hurt the business too much. After the union celebrated its victory, it had to face hard business decisions due to low sales. The union had to lay off their own members.

The attitudes of both management and the union led to the downsizing of the company. Neither side won this long fight.

Better Results

Managers need to bring the union and employees into managing the business. Management needs their ideas and enthusiasm. Be loyal to workers and treat them with respect. That respect will be returned.

Unions need to focus on benefiting their members, not getting the most income. Strikes are destructive as a negotiating tool. They hurt the union, the company, and the customers. Without customers you don't have a job.

How many months does an employee have to work to make up the income lost by striking? Before you strike, look for low impact ways to show your displeasure. How about a one shift strike? Take off one shift, protest in front of the television cameras, and resume work quickly. You have made a point but not damaged your own jobs. Actually a one or two hour strike may work just as well. Long strikes are not effective anymore in a global economy.

Successful Union Tactics

Sargent and Company wanted to implement Demand Flow Technology (Just In Time) to be competitive. The company brought union officials into the meeting with the consultants. They explained the benefits would be a more secure, competitive business employing more union members. Sargent and Company further guaranteed no union member would lose their job from implementing the changes. All personnel reduction would be from normal retirement or people moving on by themselves. Second, when the jobs became more efficient the salary of the workers would be increased to compensate for lost overtime.

The union negotiated and revised its rules to make changes. They explained the benefits to the members and brought their members' concerns to management. Management responded to the union concerns with give and take. The implementation of DFT was completed very successfully and benefitted the company, the management, and the workers. Over 80% of product was shipped in five business days compared to six to eight weeks by competitors. The result was Sargent and Company grew from number three in its market to a strong number two over the next few years. When the market went sour, their union lost less than 10% of its members. Compare that to competitors who lost 30% to 70% of their production jobs. Teamwork between companies and unions does pay off.

My Experience

For me, the strike ended after two years. My government division was operating well and they could supervise employees with less effort since they were experienced now. I tried to work in the commercial division but had apparently offended an HR personnel manager by talking about how the products could be improved. Since I competed for fun, I heard from users about their experiences and tried to get us to make better products. The personnel manager thought I was disloyal and blocked me from getting another position. A manager wanted me to work for him but I was not getting that position. So I found other work and missed the final chapter in person.

The best part was the relief I felt not having to cross the picket lines every day. The daily stress was gone. I hope and plan to never work for a striking company again.

"If you wish to achieve worthwhile things in your personal and career life, you must become a worthwhile person in your own self-development."

Brian Tracy
1944-
American Trainer, Speaker, Author, Businessman

Is There a Leader Within You?

Janet L. Newcomb and Jacqueline A. Soares

22

L eadership is a subject near and dear to our hearts. We have lived it, studied it, taught it, coached and mentored it, and watched it grow seemingly by accident. What have we learned that would be useful to you? Perhaps the best way to share these lessons would be to take you on a journey with one of our typical clients - a blend created from experiences with the many leaders we've had the pleasure to work with.

Omigosh, I'm a leader – now what?

Joe had just been promoted to vice president of a multi-million dollar company. The company gave him a coach to help him succeed in his new assignment. That was the first interesting thing we noticed – he had been promoted to a very high leadership position *before* going through the company's leadership development program. In the good old days, you started at the bottom of a company, worked your way up the ladder, gained knowledge and experience on the way, and benefited from the wisdom of many who had walked the road before you. No more. Now, young, relatively inexperienced, employees are being promoted quickly based on their education and individual performance (or assumed potential) without the benefit of the seasoning that comes with time. Joe had to get up to speed and find a way to succeed quickly because he was being watched closely – by both the president and his new peer group. We had a lot to work with, though. Joe was highly motivated, smart, personable, and definitely looked the part of a high-level executive. But where to start? What were the main things to focus on in this leadership development engagement?

A Mental Shift

Joe had been an achiever all his life. Customers loved him and he had been very successful at bringing new business into the company. He knew how to perform. Now, it was no longer about his individual performance and achievements. He had to learn how to get results through others – a different task and mindset. One of the first things we helped him see was that he needed to get to know his employees, understanding who they were and what motivated them, rather than applying a one size fits all approach to management.

He had most of the skills. It was more a matter of getting him to see the employees through the same lens he had previously applied to customers. Who were they? What was important to them? How could he meet their needs in a way that motivated them to achieve the goals he set? Joe found that the more time he invested in his employees, getting to know them as unique individuals with unique skills and motivations, the better things went. It was hard at first to break the habit of doing the work himself. He needed to practice being patient and wait for others to accomplish the goals. He spent a lot more time listening and communicating. It didn't seem like real work to him. In several months, he was delighted to find that while he was actually *doing* less work himself, his whole department was achieving far more than when we first started working with him.

Surf's Up

Joe was proud of being able to react quickly and put out the fires whenever there was a problem. He had become well known as the go-to guy at the company for any customer who had a complaint or an unusual situation that required special attention.

Now this was no longer his job. He had to learn to hand these challenges over to others and teach them how to manage emergencies effectively. It felt like having to unlearn much of what he had spent his entire career learning. He even had to let employees make their own mistakes – sometimes the most impactful way to learn. Not solving problems was definitely a problem for Joe. It created a lot of discomfort for this customer and results-oriented personality! People began to notice that Joe sometimes looked a little stressed out. This charming executive had even snapped at a few people lately.

We asked Joe what he did on a regular basis to relax and relieve stress. He told us a lot about what he used to do before he became a busy executive with a wife and three small children. It turned out he worked all day, came home late and barely had any quality time to spend with his family before he dropped into bed exhausted.

Does this sound familiar? Each day was more of the same. He also took work home on weekends so that he could keep up with all his responsibilities. He didn't see how he could make room for another commitment in his schedule.

With gentle coaxing, we helped him see that we all have only 24 hours in each day, no matter who we are. The trick is to manage that time so that our most important priorities are met on a consistent basis. It took a little longer, and some not-so-gentle coaxing, to convince him that taking care of himself and managing his own time and energy should be one of his first priorities. We gave him an assignment to begin surfing on a regular basis – and to schedule it on his calendar just like any other important meeting. No cancelling except for real unavoidable emergencies.

People began to notice something different about Joe. He didn't look as stressed. He was more patient. He made more thoughtful decisions. He just seemed generally more at ease. What was different? We decided to let them wonder – because the only thing really different was that Joe was surfing on a regular basis.

It's been our experience with many executives who are highly extroverted and kinesthetic that without a regular physical outlet it's much harder to manage stress. And once you're a high level executive, you can count on lots of stress. This one practice, learning to express and manage your energy through regular physical exercise of some kind, pays dividends many times over the amount of time actually invested. It also allows you to apply your leadership strengths in a very focused and effective way.

Leadership Strengths

Joe was a natural leader who only needed to adjust to his new role and learn to be more mindful about managing his time and energy. We are most fortunate to work with many people like Joe who are already highly successful and just need what we call fine tuning. It's exciting to watch them continue to grow. Thinking about all the leaders we have worked with, we have come to some conclusions about leadership strengths.

Regardless of how many different kinds of leaders there are or how many different kinds of challenges leaders face, we believe there are two fundamental sets of requirements for leadership. One we define as leadership *qualities*. The other we define as leadership *competencies*. Leadership *qualities* are applicable and useful in any leadership role. Leadership *competencies* are more situational and relative to the specific type of leadership role being played.

In Joe's case, the enduring leadership *qualities* he exhibited were honesty, integrity, a strong sense of justice/fairness, humility and an ability to admit mistakes, high levels of intelligence and motivation, openness to trying and learning new things, strong commitment to the company and the common good, willingness to share credit with others, sincere interest in people and their development, and a willingness to confront rather than avoid difficult issues.

Joe's strongest *competencies* were his ability to imagine, envision and articulate a desired future, innovative thinking, creative problem solving, and calculated risk taking. He was also adept at reading nonverbal signals and connecting quickly with others to build harmonious relationships in support of common goals. He motivated others by generously sharing his own excitement, enthusiasm, and support for various projects. He was also an effective logical and critical thinker with well-defined intentions and the ability to fashion cost-effective strategies for any situation. Detail and discipline were not well developed competencies; however, at his level they were not such important requirements because he had employees he could rely on to provide strength in these areas. He was actually very well matched to his new job and got along very well.

Is leadership your gig?

Do you aspire to be a leader? Are you well suited to the role? How will you know? We have observed that the most effective leaders have demonstrated natural inclinations toward leadership from a very early age. Were you the kid in your neighborhood who set up the lemonade stand on the corner? Did the other kids follow you when you suggested new things to try or new places to explore? Do you actually enjoy being responsible for the accomplishments of others or would you prefer to be an in-depth expert on a more narrowly defined subject?

Leadership can be a challenging role. We believe it shouldn't be attempted unless you are well suited for the role and actually desire to make a serious commitment to the challenges involved. Assessment instruments can be helpful in determining your natural strengths and weaknesses and the extent of your competency development in various areas. One of the best we have found is the Benziger Thinking Styles Assessment (BTSA). You can read more about this instrument at www.focusedcoach.com or Dr. Benziger's website at www.benziger.org

Conclusions

Some of the best leaders are extroverted and creative risk takers, imaginative, passionate, and people oriented. They have a clear vision about where they are headed and are able to convince others they have the wherewithal to get there. They can make quick decisions when need be, but prefer to orchestrate consensus when there's time. We understand that there's quite a debate between nature and nurture when it comes to leadership – we tend to believe it's some of both. Natural inclinations and talents, coupled with the right opportunities and good coaches/mentors along the way, seems to be the most successful and enduring recipe for leadership no matter what the time or place.

So You Want To Be a
Business Owner

23

Janet L. Newcomb & Michael D. Hardesty

A t some point in many people's lives, the thought of having their own business occurs to them. Sometimes it's just a daydream, a chance for a mental escape, however briefly, from current corporate pressures. Sometimes it's a long term plan they are beginning to formulate, to implement at a later time, possibly after retirement from their current job. And sometimes it's a current reality - you're ready to get started down a new path. Never having done this before, what are the most important things to consider?

What kind of business owner will you be?

There are a number of ways to own a business and pros and cons associated with each. It's important to think about what you enjoy, what you are good at, how much money you have to invest and what else will be needed to be successful. Here's a brief outline of some things to consider:

Sole Practitioner
Pros
- Prestige – You can become an expert in your chosen area of service.

163

- Maximum freedom and control – you make all the decisions and there are no employees to supervise.

Cons

- Everything depends on you. If you're not working, there is no business.
- Your earning potential may be limited.
- Life balance issues may arise if too much of your identity and time is wrapped up in your business.

Entrepreneur – Designing and creating a whole new business
Pros

- Creative control and personal satisfaction - you decide what business you are in, what it will look like and how it will be run.
- Freedom and Flexibility - you are the boss – you make the decisions. You can decide when, where and how to do your work.
- Variety – entrepreneurs must wear many hats, usually very appealing to an entrepreneurial personality.

Cons

- The buck stops with you – in the beginning, you have total responsibility for results.
- Until you can afford to hire employees, there's no one to help you! So you may be working more hours than when you had a job.
- There are no guarantees you will make money. Be prepared financially and emotionally for this to take longer than you anticipated.
- Even if you are very good at what you do, you may not really understand how to run or grow a business.
- There's no structure like you may have been used to in a corporation – you must create it.

- If your family's not supportive, you'll need to be prepared to address the conflicts.

Franchisee – Managing someone else's business design

There's a free resource available to help you decide if owning a franchise is right for you.

It's called FranNet. Their consultants look at your background, help you understand whether franchising is a good fit for you, and then connect you with one or more franchises that could be a good match. Take a look at www.frannet.com.

In the meantime, here are a few things we'd recommend you consider:

Pros
- You don't have to create the business concept – that's already done for you.
- The franchisor is actively building the brand at a more global level, creating value and making it easier for you to sell your product or service at the local level.
- You receive training in how to run the business.
- Marketing materials and management systems are already designed.
- You have a support system in place for advice and counsel as you grow.
- The franchisor tends to track market trends, do research and assume responsibility for creating new products and services for the franchise.

Cons
- Initial investment may be high.
- You have to share your profits/royalties with the franchisor.
- You are limited regarding the number and kinds of changes you can make to the business.

Buyer of Existing Business
Pros

- You're in business right away. Someone else started the business and the status quo should remain, initially.
- Immediate cash flow. If inventories and accounts receivable are in place, you can generate income from the first day.
- Customer base is already in place. Vendors and customers are there and previous relationships exist.
- Less competition. Buying a business may eliminate a competitor that you might have had if you started a business from scratch.
- Easier financing. Because the business has a track record, financing should be easier.

Cons

- There may be inherent problems in the business, some which may not become known until <u>after</u> the sale.
- Out-of-date inventories may have to be sold at markdown prices. Costly.
- Bad debt possibilities. Some of the accounts receivable (often much of the accounts receivable) may not be collectable. The Balance Sheet is often inflated for purposes of making the sale.
- Since sellers always have an inflated perception of the value of their company, it may be more costly to buy an existing business than start one from the ground up.
- The seller is a problem. He was a different person during the negotiations but after the deal is done, Mr. Hyde rears his ugly self and becomes difficult to deal with.

What's required to have a successful business?

There are many elements driving a successful business. They tend to fall into three distinct areas:

- The people stuff
- The financial stuff
- The operational stuff

However, the most important element is planning. Plan the work and work the plan.

Systems, policies and procedures must be understood and implemented. Following close behind are assigning responsibility and accountability. Ignore the basics and you can become part of the 80% that don't make it. Refuse to lose!

Once you are a business owner, what's important to know about managing a business?

Regardless of business form, our many years of experience have shown us that good managers share many similarities that contribute to their success. Here are some tips to keep you focused on the most important characteristics to have, acquire or develop:

Recognize that it is people, not structural changes, which make an organization work or fail. Organizational change alone is not the answer. Good talented people who are dedicated can make almost any organizational structure succeed.

Provide for a successor. Every manager should have a backup person who is potentially qualified to perform his/her job. If there is no one who has this potential, then you must give top priority to training someone who does.

Deal with tenure problems fairly and candidly. Some individuals who have long, distinguished records of service in the company reach a point where their job responsibilities move beyond their energy level or capabilities. The manager and the organization both have an obligation to those people who have served it loyally. If they can no longer pull their own weight, however, they have to be removed from the mainstream.

Communicate expectations ... Measure performance, act on results. Rewards should be for achieving results, not effort.

Don't accept marginal performance. The most frequent and insidious mistake managers make is to live too long with marginal or poor performance. The capable manager must be tough minded in his/her performance evaluations. The manager must be unemotional when making decisions as to who can perform and who cannot and be eminently fair and decisive in the way decisions are carried out.

Criticize only in private. Criticism should be saved for private discussion enabling the manager to handle the problem or correct matters with his/her subordinates in private.

Weed out misfits. People in an organization invariably know who the misfits are and will quickly draw negative conclusions about the manager's own ability if he/she permits them to stay.

Cultivate individual ambition and drive while encouraging a team orientation. Individuals should not be criticized because they are too ambitious, too aggressive, or too impatient, as long as he/she is a good thinker, fair and straightforward in his/her dealing and actions with others, and committed to the company's goals as well as his/her own.

Focus objectively on personal accomplishments, not personal differences. A manager must understand that race, age, sex, heritage, and socio-cultural characteristics have nothing whatsoever to do with evaluating an individual's effectiveness in a company.

Let people know their status and prospects. A manager should ensure that people in the organization know their performance measurements and what their career outlook is at all times--- even if it hurts.

Provide training, but stress self-development. A company can point the way and assist with company-sponsored educational and training programs, but self-development is the key to success. Each person must shoulder that management responsibility on his or her own.

Create and maintain an attractive, healthy company environment. This last ground rule sums up all the previous guidelines. It underscores the essential responsibility of a manager to provide people in the organization with a situation and an opportunity to work effectively in a common effort, develop their capabilities, fulfill their professional aspirations, and achieve appropriate recognition and rewards.

"I am looking for a lot of men who have an infinite capacity to not know what can't be done."

Henry Ford
1863-1947
American Automobile Manufacturer

Mental Preparation for Owning a Business

24

Lee Pound

Many people leave corporate positions thinking that it will be easy to start a business. After all, they have years of experience in upper management, they've got all the right degrees, and they know how to hire and fire.

They announce to the world that they are now consultants, coaches, speakers, writers, or widget manufacturers. They might get involved in multi-level marketing or become an independent contractor.

These newly minted businesspersons quickly find out that there is more to running a business than just saying you are in business. In fact, businesses such as this fail at an alarming rate.

Corporate Mindset vs. Entrepreneurial Mindset

In many ways, working for a large corporation insulates middle and upper management from many of the pressures of running a business in a number of ways:

- Jobs tend to be highly stratified by function.
- Most managers are more concerned with day-to-day functions than with strategic planning.

171

- Most managers have minimal experience in sales.
- Jobs tend to be highly structured and defined by numerous written policies.
- Most managers must answer to a superior one step up the corporate ladder.
- The reward for good performance is an increase in salary or promotion to the next level of responsibility.
- Retirement comes at age 65, no matter what.

Starting a business, particularly a small company, involves a different set of skills.

- The small business owner is first and foremost a salesman.
- The owner creates the vision, sets policies, hires and fires, and can't pass the blame onto a superior.
- The owner will see no promotions or pay increases except through his or her own efforts.
- Jobs tend to be minimally structured.
- Every person in the company may perform two or three or more different tasks.

The Keys to Success

Given these fundamental differences, how should a recent graduate of corporate America approach starting a business?

Based on my experience starting and running several businesses, there are basic steps that every new entrepreneur must take before opening the doors. These steps will increase exponentially the prospect of creating a successful business.

1. Create a detailed vision of your future company.

When my business partner and I created the Speak Your Way to Wealth seminars, we worked for almost a year just on the conceptual framework. By the end of that year, we knew exactly what type of seminar we would create, the type of speakers we would invite, the target audience, the marketing methods we would use, and what the event would look like on opening day.

2. Believe that your company will succeed.

A lot has been written about the power of belief. I am not talking here about blind belief but about being comfortable with the idea that you have a product that people want to buy, that will help them succeed, and that will make a vast difference in their lives.

When you eliminate doubt and fear, you can move with confidence toward creating the company you desire. This doesn't mean that you won't have setbacks. You will. It means that you learn from the problems and adjust to ensure your future success.

3. Don't be afraid to ask for help.

Too many new entrepreneurs think they know it all. In fact, the first thing you should do is find a mentor. Then you should join a professional organization. If you have questions, seek out someone who has been there. Don't reinvent. Learn from those who have gone before.

When we started the seminar company, we knew very little about how to put on a major event. At each major step we found the answers to our questions from professionals who were more than happy to help.

4. Take constant, steady action to build your company.

After deciding to form the seminar company, we took one step that made everything else possible. We simply agreed to talk every Monday morning at 10 a.m. for an hour. This forced us to discuss the event, to make decisions, and to start organizing.

We found that when we were talking, new ideas would flow, new possibilities would surface, we would ask potential speakers to join us on the platform, in other words, we would take one more step toward creating our new reality.

5. Act as if you are successful.

As we created the seminar business, we introduced ourselves as seminar producers, and we talked about the event as if it already existed. We didn't say we wanted to put on an event, or that we wanted to be seminar producers. We were.

This means we were committed to putting on the event, just as you need to be committed to making your business happen. If that commitment does not exist, you may as well not bother.

6. Don't let anyone talk you out of success.

You'll hear a lot of negative talk from those who do not want you to succeed. It may come from family, friends, former co-workers, neighbors, or potential customers. If you believe fully in your idea for your business, you will make it happen in spite of the negative talk.

7. Become a salesperson.

Most of your time will be spent selling. Your job as the owner of a business is to get customers. Without them you will find it impossible to succeed. Find the best sales training you can get and learn everything you possibly can.

Conclusion

It is possible to go from corporate life to entrepreneurship and succeed. You just need the right mindset, the determination to make your business grow, and belief in your vision for the future.

Section Three

Advanced Career Tactics

"We are all of us stars and we all deserve to twinkle."

Marilyn Monroe
1926-1962
American Actress

Career Development in Business and Industry

25

John Hall

T his chapter addresses career planning and development in the workplace. I will review the recent evolution of several career planning and development models and then describe how a career planning and development program benefits an organization and its employees. I will describe several career planning and guidance objectives which are proving themselves effective in business and industry. I begin with the varying perspectives on career planning and development.

The Employee

In an organization, the responsibility and function of the career counselor can vary greatly, depending on the perspective of the individual examining the issue. Most employees will view career counseling as a means of identifying and navigating career paths within the organization. They ask questions such as: Is there a ladder to climb? How do I get promoted? How do I get the skills that will get me ahead? Is there training that I can get in the company? When can I make a move?

At this level most men and women want to do something in the next year. To these employees, career development is synonymous with upward mobility.

The Supervisor
The supervisor sees career development as a way to motivate and direct employees in their daily tasks. They are likely to view helping employees make choices as positive only if those choices benefit their department. While they are in an ideal position to assess, counsel, and coach the employee for optimal career development, many supervisors view this as one more time-consuming task dictated by management whim. Nevertheless, many large organizations employ counselors to provide career counseling to supervisors so that they can effectively guide the careers of their employees.

Top Management
Top management will be focusing on the big picture so their time frame will be longer, typically five to seven years. They will think of the career counselor as a succession planning expert. They are interested in identifying who the potential managers are among their employees. They will also want to know if those managers and other key people have the right skills to move into top jobs. Top managers are interested in learning how to train the fast track managers and to pinpoint when they will be ready to move into key positions. For some organizations, career planning programs are used as a way to facilitate the departure of individuals whose long-term potential is not within the organization.

The Evolving Models of Career Development
Because of Equal Employment Opportunity and Affirmative Action programs in the 1960's and 1970's, many companies hired guidance counselors to recruit minority workers. They counseled women and minorities about the

promotional opportunities within the organization and guided them through the educational and political steps that might lead to higher-level positions. The first career development programs used in business and industry in the 1960's and 1970's were individually focused. They put a lot of attention on the individual's motivation, self actualization, growth, and development. They included humanistic psychology into the methods and focused a lot on Maslow's Hierarchy of Needs. Employees were given company sponsored training that may or may not have had an impact on the organization.

In the 1970's companies moved into organizational models of career development. A direct opposite of the individual model which allowed all employees to develop their career potential, this model directed the employee's career path. They often did career development only for the fast track employees, attempting to create structured career path systems for them. Assessment centers were used primarily to assess managerial skills.

An organization has to make a profit or it will go out of business, but the individual needs to develop and grow in ways consistent with their values and skills. Ideally, career development in the workplace allows individuals at all levels to maximize their career development and at the same time maximize the bottom line of the company. Therefore, by the late 1970's and the early 1980's, there was a movement toward a partnership model. In this model career development is seen as a joint venture between the organization, the supervisor, and the employee. The organization provides materials, resources, a room, and career counseling. The employee provides the direction and energy for career development. Much of the success of this model depends on training supervisors in counseling skills. Top management likes this model because they see it as succession planning. Middle management buys into this model because they see career development as being tied into all other parts of human resources, as well as being a management development system. The supervisor sees it as a tool that helps them motivate their employees using counseling skills. And finally the employee sees it as an upward mobility tool.

The Promotion Trap

All companies are staffed with professionals who are confronting the choice of becoming managers or remaining in their professional or technical tracks. They are uncertain whether they possess management skills or whether they would find the role of manager satisfying. They will confront the career counselor with questions like: How will a management position affect my lifestyle? Will I miss my technical work? How can I acquire management skills?

If they make the wrong decision, it can damage the organization and devastate the individual's career. Even in those companies that have dual track compensation systems there are a lot of messages that convey that being a manager is more prestigious.

The technically trained man or woman sometimes falls victim to this kind of promotion trap. For example, the skilled engineer moves to a managerial position. However, the result is often an excellent engineer becoming a poor engineering manager. Typically the engineer will stay in a management position three to four years, making all sorts of mistakes. During those years their staff gets lousy management which sometimes results in several staff members quitting. During their exit interview they will identify their reason for quitting as poor management. After this happens several times the engineering manager becomes a candidate for outplacement. Unfortunately, there is a lot of damage before the company deals with the poor manager. Huge amounts of money are involved when the wrong person is promoted to management. It can easily cost $45,000 in replacement costs.

There is a fee for a head hunter, fees to advertise in the Wall Street Journal, down time when no one is in place, and costs to train a new manager. All this does not even address the people who were poorly managed for three or four years.

The Frustrated Secretary

Many secretaries and clerical workers feel blocked from moving into professional positions. They want to know if there is a bridge job in the organization where they can move over to a professional area. Society is telling her (it is usually a her) that she ought to be a professional and she is angry because there is no apparent way for her to become a professional. This block may stem from the absence of real bridge jobs or simply from a lack of knowledge on the secretary's part. An effective career and development program should target this population in its design.

The Plateaued Professional

A career development program must deal with professional men and women who are plateaued in their careers, men and women who have lost touch with their motivated skills and creativity. It isn't unusual for a man or a woman professional as they move into middle-age to find the range of their opportunities narrowing and ambitions becoming thwarted while still years from retirement. Today in most industries this plateauing begins at 42 and is trending downward. The first hint of plateauing may be exclusion from a company trip to another facility for training on new methods and technologies. Then a Catch-22 is set up where they are denied promotion because they lack the skills to do the job. Because they have been so isolated they usually have no idea that anybody else has the same problems or is going through a similar mid-life crisis. A career development program can reconnect these plateaued professionals with their skills and talents.

High-Tech Musical Chairs

Highly visible employees often present career and development problems for themselves and their companies. Usually they have advanced degrees in computer science or engineering and earn over $70,000 a year. They are the prey of the headhunter and may have made three or more job changes in the last few years. They may already have two BMWs and a nice home and are beginning to wonder if there is anything else important to accomplish both personally and in their careers. Their career choices and stability are important to companies because it costs a fortune when they change jobs. Companies pay a 30 percent headhunter fee, usually in excess of $25.000. Then there are advertising fees and down time. It is evident that you can pay for a career development program by getting one or two of these much sought after people to focus within the company.

Conclusion

Space limitations do not permit my detailing the full range of career planning and development in business and industry. Other areas I could have touched upon are employees approaching retirement, the injured worker, and technological change and its effects on career and development. It is my hope that, as we move into the 21st century, organizations will use more career planning and development to decrease turnover and make the best use of their human resources.

References

Bardwick,]. M. (1986). *The Plateauing Trap*. New York: American Management Association

Brown, D., Brooks, L. (1984). *Career Choice and Development*. San Francisco: Jossey-Bass

Gysbers, N. C., (1984). *Designing Careers* San Francisco: Jossey-Bass

Know dell, R. L., McDaniels, C., Hesser, A., and Walz, B. (19 83). *Outplacement Counseling*. Ann Arbor: ERIC/CAPS.

The Five Stages of Job Loss

26

John Hall

Job loss is unlike any other loss: it is a sudden, brutal destruction of self-esteem. It triggers a series of psychological stages similar to the stages of dying described by Kubler-Ross in her book *On Death and Dying*. The speed at which people pass through these phases varies greatly. However, these negative phases of job loss actually perform a positive function. The stages are:

1. Shock
2. Fear
3. Anger and blame
4. Shame
5. Despair

Shock

Shock, the first stage of failure, is characterized by an initial state of numbness and disbelief; the mind denies what it cannot process. Numbness then gives way to awareness of a terrible blow at which time a random event might punctuate the numbness and trigger sudden weeping. At this stage we are liable to draw strange conclusions and behave in odd ways. We are struggling to absorb a blow. Whenever shock occurs, it is safer to do absolutely nothing except wait and allow the pain to recede.

When you are in the stage of shock, what you need most is a sympathetic listener, not someone who will offer advice, someone to sympathize with the injustice and be furious with you, someone who says, "Those bastards! How did they do that to you?"

Fear

Close on the heels of shock is fear. The fears may be appropriate: (How will I pay the mortgage? How will I meet my children's school bills? What will I tell so-and-so when he calls?). But they can escalate quickly to unmanageable proportions (What if I never work again? Suppose nobody ever calls me?)

To those who have lost their jobs, fear is a multifaceted enemy, almost impossible to grasp. The task is to break it down into a manageable size, to confront only one terror at a time. Fear needs to be taken out of the shadows, where it is always more terrifying than in the light of day, by looking at it not as one giant problem but as a set of discrete issues for which solutions can be found. Fear can become manageable. For some people an inner approach, using meditation, is helpful. For others, confronting their fears one at a time brings relief.

Anger and Blame

Anger is appropriate; it is a sign that you value yourself. It is so appropriate that corporations pay vast sums of money to outplacement counselors to defuse employees' anger. They don't want you bad-mouthing or stealing from them. Anger can also lead to sleeplessness, irritability, and a constant sense of frustration.

Almost everyone who loses a job indulges in fantasy.

These fantasies can be both satisfying and therapeutic. Nevertheless, be careful of acting from a desire for revenge. Once your hot anger has subsided, a sense of cool outrage can be extremely useful.

Almost everyone engages in blame after losing his or her job. Blame is a perfectly logical response: something or someone had to cause this annihilation of us. Sometimes we blame ourselves instead of others. How could our judgment have been so wrong? Why *were* we dumb enough to let this happen to us? Why didn't I get out in time?

Blame will be your first interpretation, but it is almost always inaccurate. Causality is always more complicated than it seems on the surface and upon objective evaluation it may also be true that you had some interpersonal input that played a part as well. Feelings of blame serve a definite function; they allow us to see the world as a place ruled by order rather than chance. Blame becomes a problem only if it becomes persistent.

Shame

Shame owes its existence to the authority we give other people to judge us. "What will they think of us?" is a question we have been programmed from childhood to ask ourselves. Most of the time, we don't even know who they are.

After you lose a job, some people may approach you cautiously, in a probing manner. In a nervous manner, they might ask, "Are you all right?" This is a moment of great opportunity. Your attitude about yourself will determine the way they see you. You are in power here and can program the way others think of you. Failure is not a mark of shame unless you act ashamed.

If ever there is a time for deception, it is during the stage of shame. Save your true feelings for your family and one or two close friends; when facing the career world, it is smarter to wear a mask. To combat any sense of shame, develop a short, well-rehearsed speech that emphasizes the future.

Sometimes people are so fearful of others' opinions they refuse to take a lesser job. They let their own sense of shame get in the way of what could be an opportunity. Sometimes you may have to be willing to go backward before you can go forward. Activity, at any level, begets another activity and is the best antidote to shame.

Depression

You don't necessarily become depressed upon losing your job. You may be shocked, angry, or fearful, but as long as you believe in your own worth (self-esteem) and as long as you believe in your ability to provide a better future (self-confidence), you will not fall into depression. Depression occurs only when there is an ego loss with no subsequent ego gain and no apparent way out.

If an artist loses his/her job as a waiter he is unlikely to feel depression. He merely lost a job. If on the other hand, your job and your life are one and the same, the loss will lead to a deep depression.

Depression usually sets in sixty to ninety days after the loss of a job if there are no strong prospects for another position. The good news, however, is that most depression is self-limiting. No matter what you do - whether you see a psychiatrist, go jogging, or do nothing - unless you are mentally ill, after a period of a few months, at most, the depression will usually run its course.

One of the best ways to hasten the end of this stage of depression is to give into it and allow yourself to mourn.

Use a Proposal to Land A Great Job

27

John Hall

B en Hembree, a 32-year-old marketing manager, began his campaign for a marketing position like everyone else, by mailing hundreds of resumes and cover letters, and got the same result as almost everyone else - nothing.

Hembree states, "After two hundred mailings with zero responses, I decided I had three options: poverty, crime, or finding a more effective approach to the job market. Rejecting poverty and crime, I got actively involved in several industry associations, did in-depth research on the food industry, and read every current business article I could get my hands on. My research and industry networking helped me develop an understanding of where the problems/opportunities were and to position myself as a problem solver."

Hembree adds, "I then selected six companies to target and prepared a forty page marketing program, complete with charts and graphs, which I hoped demonstrated that I had the marketing savvy to increase their bottom lines. My proposal resulted in two offers, both from companies which had earlier failed to respond to my resumes and cover letters."

Ben Hembree's success resulted from abandoning reactive job search methods for the more proactive techniques used by successful consultants.

Think like a consultant.

"Consultative techniques directly apply to management level job searches," says Ron Smith, a management consultant in Tustin, California who has worked with many Fortune 500 companies and is an adjunct professor of Human Resources at San Diego based National University.

Smith adds, "The analogy is straightforward. A management consultant has to do a lot of research, interview key industry people, and then sell himself to the company. Isn't this exactly what someone looking for a management position should be doing?"

William Moody, a Torrance, California, management consultant and trainer, feels job seekers should approach target companies as change agents.

Moody states, "Management level job hunters need to research target companies and assess their status quo, where those companies want to be, and where they could be in the next few years. The only way I know to do this is by the same type of in-depth research a successful consultant must do to land corporate contracts."

Proposals

In today's world of downsizing, right sizing, mergers, acquisitions, re-engineering, re-structuring, off shore manufacturing, bankruptcies, foreign competition, and an economy which is moving ahead with the speed of a herd of turtles, management and executive level job hunters must separate themselves from the pack. Because less than one in a thousand job hunters uses them, proposals are an excellent way to do this.

Alan Landry, who teaches marketing management at Pepperdine University's Executive MBA program, feels that developing a proposal for a targeted company is Basic undergraduate Marketing 101: find a need and fill it.

"In the dramatically downsizing business environment we are in," Landry states, "companies are not interested in just warm bodies with MBA's but are demanding individuals who can get things done."

Tom Jackson, in his book *Guerrilla Tactics in the New Job Market* (Bantam Books 1991) writes, "The mere fact that you are willing to demonstrate an interest and ability in the area will put you ahead of most others, whose primary communication to employers is need and dependency."

"Proposal opportunities are not difficult to develop for an informed individual," says Dan Gilliland, a career coach in Orange County, California. Gilliland advises job hunters to "Look for events that represent changes taking place in an organization that fall within their functional areas. Several years ago I worked with a client whose area of expertise was finance. My client read an article in *The Orange County Business Journal* about a small computer company which was planning to go public. He sent the company a two-page proposal indicating how he could save it thousands of dollars with their initial public offering. In his proposal he detailed how his experience helping two similar companies through the process would directly benefit them. Two days after dropping the proposal in the mail he got a call from the company's president, who wanted to talk. My client was hired on a six month consulting basis which led to a full-time controller position at another company."

Gilliland adds, "He saw a need and clearly demonstrated how he could fill it. Unfortunately, far too many men and women miss job opportunities, not through lack of ability or experience, but because they fail to stay informed."

Kathleen Jennings, president of the Jennings Company, a Seattle, Washington, based executive marketing and outplacement company suggests asking "what if" when looking for a proposal topic.

Jennings recalls a client from ten years ago. "He was frustrated that his 25 years of experience in managed health care was perceived as overqualified. Adapting a consultative approach, he focused on a company which had a flat organizational structure with eight managers reporting to the CEO. He developed a proposal based on the concept 'what if' the CEO were free for business development. His proposal suggested that a position be created, Vice President of Operations, which would take over many of the operational systems and day to day business of the CEO. The proposal was presented to corporate offices in Texas and won approval after a relatively short time." Jennings adds, "The implementation was a grand slam success. He began work in an organization with three offices and eighty employees that has grown, in three years, to six offices and 160 employees."

Getting Inside the Company

There are several approaches to getting proposals into the hands of hiring managers at target companies. I tell my clients that "using a proposal, it is possible to develop and land a position in companies ranging in size from start-up to about $10 million without an inside contact. However, once a company grows beyond $10 million, you need to know someone on the inside."

William Moody advises job hunters to use professional and trade associations to develop inside contacts. Moody suggests that "a CPA targeting a specific company should find out what industry organizations the CFO belongs to and attend a few meetings. Just a few minutes with that CFO may enable him to get a proposal seriously considered in the company."

It is relatively easy to submit a proposal following either an information or job interview. Job hunters can accomplish this by approaching every interview the way a consultant approaches a company; that is, be prepared to give a verbal proposal of how you will bring added value to the organization. Then be willing to follow up with a written proposal. An easy way to do this is to mention in your thank you letter that you "have some ideas which might be helpful concerning our discussion on .... ," then mentioning the area in which you want to do a proposal. Finally add, "I'll call you in a few days to run my ideas past you." When you call say something like, "If you would be interested, I'll put my thoughts in writing." Most managers will agree to this, hence giving your proposal an excellent chance of being seriously reviewed.

One Proposal, Several Companies

A common objection to creating a proposal for a company is that it's a lot of work without any assurance of landing a position. However, word processing makes it relatively easy to modify a proposal any number of times during a job campaign.

For example, Victor Alvarez, a 42-year-old facilities manager, wrote a 15-page proposal for The University of California San Diego, which was based on in-depth research and network contacts. As a result, he was one of two final candidates for the position.

Even though he did not land the job, his proposal was not wasted as he modified it for a position as a facilities manager at a California State University campus, where he was offered and accepted a position. Alvarez also modified it for a large national transportation company headquartered in Dallas, where he was one of the final candidates before accepting the university position. Mr. Alvarez writes, "Selecting the topic was the most difficult part of the process. However, with a few questions to industry contacts and some research I was able to determine the likelihood of my topic being of value. Word processing made modifying it several times easy. The rest was simple: organize and word process the proposal, have it professionally bound, and send it off to the decision-makers."

But I'll give away the store.

An objection often heard by management level job hunters when presented with the concept of writing a proposal is a fear of giving away the store.

"While that is a small possibility, it is far more likely that you will be perceived as someone with initiative, insight, and real world savvy," says Dave Swanson, a career consultant in Milwaukee, Wisconsin, who gives more than sixty college and university seminars a year based on Richard Bolle's *What Color Is Your Parachute* (10 Speed Press, revised annually).

Swanson continues, "I believe 'giving away the store' thinking damages job search and long term career growth. Some years ago, I was looking for a position with a college or university in the Milwaukee area. A friend introduced me to the vice president of a local community college, who explained over lunch some of the academic and career direction issues with which they were dealing. Based on information I gathered at that luncheon and on researching the college, I was able to put together a forty-page proposal which contained over sixty new ideas."

Mr. Swanson goes on, "The College could have taken any of the ideas and implemented them without me but because they saw that I had the expertise, experience, and savvy to come up with them, they concluded it was only logical to have me implement them, and a position, Director of Career Services, was created for me."

Management consultant Ron Smith agrees with Dave Swanson and adds, "The sharper the management team in a company, the more likely a well thought out proposal will land its author a position. It is this simple. Any company that plans on being around a long time must think in terms of succession planning, i.e. 'We are more likely to survive and grow if we hire and encourage men and women with initiative, insight and brains.'" Mr. Smith adds, "Therefore approaching companies with a well thought out proposal that focuses on a clear win-win for both the company and the author puts individuals light years ahead of typical job hunters."

Elements of a Good Proposal

A proposal does not have to have an original concept. It only needs to demonstrate that the job hunter has the savvy to bring added value to the targeted organization. The length can vary considerably from just a few pages to fifty or more and may include charts and graphs. A good proposal typically includes:

- **A Transmittal Letter** which presents the writer's report to the executive most involved with the problem or situation being addressed. The transmittal letter typically gives the conclusion and the highlights of the proposal.
- **A Title Page** with the title of the proposal, the name and title of the executive it is directed to, the organization, the author's name, the author's city, state and the date the proposal is being submitted.
- **A Table of Contents** which includes page numbers and should in effect present an outline consisting of all major headings and subheadings in the proposal.
- **An Executive Summary,** which is a brief, one-page summary of the proposal. Writing this will test the writer's ability to consolidate ideas and may be the only part a busy executive reads. Therefore, it should include a definition of the problem, a description of

the sources used, some highlights of the writer's ideas, and a conclusion.

- **A First Page,** which is an introduction to the proposal describing the problem/situation the writer is addressing, the methods he plans to employ, and sources consulted.

- **The Body** of the proposal should avoid using the pronouns I and we and minimize the use of *the writer, the investigator,* and *the author* and should be written naturally about things in the order in which they happened, are happening, or will happen.

- **A Concluding Section** which states the writer's conclusions but is devoted primarily to summarizing the reason for those conclusions.

Five Action Elements of Winning Proposals

1. **Research everything about the industry and its organizations**. Analyze how individual companies can reduce costs and deliver products and services better or faster. Assess their status quo—where they want to be, and where they could be in the next few years.

2. **Think like a consultant.** A management consultant conducts a lot of information interviews with key industry people and in the process develops inside relationships. This is exactly what someone looking for a management position should be doing.

3. **Look for problems, not jobs**. There isn't a company anywhere that does not have problems. Even if a company has no formal job opening, there is a good chance they have a problem that is an opportunity for you to present a proposal demonstrating that you have the savvy and initiative to solve the problem.

4. **Modify your proposal for multiple companies**. Proposals don't have to be one-shot deals. In a well-focused job search the companies you approach are

likely to have similar problems. Therefore you can modify your proposal many times. Word-processing makes such modifications relatively quick and easy.

5. **Turn job and informational interviews into proposal opportunities**. In your thank you letter, write "I have some ideas which might be helpful concerning our discussion on...." Follow up the letter with a telephone call and say; "If you'd be interested, I'd be glad to put my thoughts into a proposal for you."

"Dig the well before you are thirsty."

Chinese Proverb

Trade Associations: Gold Mines of Opportunity

28

John Hall

Brett Kayzar, a 32-year-old operations manager with 10 years of experience at a large Southern California aerospace company and who recently completed his M.B.A., wants to make a dramatic career change. His goal is to oversee the construction of exhibits as director of a zoo.

While researching opportunities, Kayzar learned about the American Association of Zoological Parks and Aquariums (AAZPA) and immediately joined the organization. Doing so gave him instant access to a wealth of information, including newsletters and membership directories. Most important, it allowed him to attend events where key personnel in the zoological industry meet.

"The access that AAZPA gave me to industry leaders made making contacts easy," says Kayzar. "As a result of these contacts, I'm now a candidate for my dream job at one of the nation's major zoological parks."

As Kayzar discovered, industry and professional associations are among the most powerful career boosters available. Yet, incredibly, few managers and professionals make use of them. Most never even bother to join a

197

professional organization - and of those who do, only a few do more than read its newsletter and occasionally attend meetings. The bottom line is this: professionals who aren't actively involved in an industry association are shortchanging their careers and missing a gold mine of opportunity.

Joining an organization strictly for the purpose of being able to say that you're a member carries little value. The most successful professionals are active in their organizations through regular attendance, program leadership and participation, mentorship of other professionals, and board, committee, and task-force participation.

Active participants are the first to learn about openings in their field, are more likely to have inside contacts at hiring companies, and are approached more often by executive search firms. In fact, Mark Fierle, a recruiter in southern California, says he often finds qualified candidates through professional organizations.

"Recently, I was able to fill a highly specialized request for a credit manager by contacting the local chapter of the National Association of Credit Managers," Mr. Fierle explains. "Professional organizations know what recruiters are talking about when we have specialized needs and can direct us to qualified members."

Associations are also the best places to effectively network with top-level professionals. When you attend events and work on committee projects, you'll naturally develop relationships with some of the most successful executives in your field - people who might not return your calls under different circumstances. In addition, if you impress these leaders with your work, they may steer you to your next career move.

Getting Started

Whatever your field, an organization exists that can help you locate job openings and gain higher visibility. The

Encyclopedia of Associations, published by Gale Research and available at most public libraries and the Internet, lists more than 23,000 professional and trade organizations, along with their addresses and phone numbers. Once you've identified associations that seem appropriate, write or call to get information on local chapters. Also check the business section of local newspapers. They contain listings of meeting times and locations for professional organizations, trade shows and conventions.

The two basic tools you'll need for your first meeting are a pen and a supply of business cards. If you're between jobs, get 1,000 business cards printed at a discount office-supply outlet. They should include your name, address, phone number, career field, any graduate degrees or professional certifications you've earned and, if you like, a sales slogan (i.e. "Excellence in after-market product sales since 1974"). Once you've joined a professional organization, you may want to add its logo to your business card to further improve your professional image. The total cost should be about $30.

Many organizations schedule an hour or so of networking before their formal meetings begin so plan to arrive early. Since attendees share a common professional interest, you'll find that starting conversations is easy.

Act like a host or hostess, not like a guest. Think about the role a host or hostess plays. They make people comfortable. You can do the same thing no matter where you are.

After you've spoken with someone for about five minutes, initiate an exchange of business cards. Then, on the back of their card, write down what author Harvey Mackay calls a WOW, something unique about the person that will help you remember him or her. Strive to meet and exchange cards with three to five members before the meeting begins. At meals, establish yourself as a friendly, take-charge leader by introducing yourself to, shaking hands with and exchanging business cards with everyone at your table. A day or two after any event, carefully go through the cards you received. Then call or write a short note to anyone you'd like to make a part of your permanent professional network.

Professional organizations depend on volunteer help. Even as a new member, you can become active immediately by volunteering for a committee. The membership committee usually is a good choice because it gives you peer-level access to people and companies in your industry.

"Also consider activities that can increase your profile in the organization, such as writing an article for the newsletter, giving a presentation, or organizing a special event," says Robert Chesney, the Irvine, California executive producer and host of *Window On Wall Street*, a business program on cable TV.

"Active participation in an industry association is essential in today's very competitive environment because exposure to industry leaders is the most direct route to positioning for continued career growth," says Chesney, who has served as president of his local Sales and Marketing Executives chapter.

Many professional organizations sponsor conventions and trade shows which are attended by industry leaders from across the nation. Susan RoAne, the San Francisco-based author of *How To Work A Room*, (1988, Warner Books) calls these meetings the Olympics of networking because they typically feature hundreds of events - seminars, cocktail parties, dinners, lunches, individual encounters, workshops and other activities - all crammed into the space of a few days to a week.

For anyone who wishes to compete for a new job professionally, attending such events is critical, says Richard Knowdell, president of Career Research & Testing, a career services firm in San Jose, California, and the editor of a newsletter for career counselors.

"National professional meetings are such a valuable resource for serious job seekers and goal-oriented professionals that I recommend borrowing the money to attend if necessary," he says.

Think Long-Term

Within three months of joining a professional organization, you can develop and nurture an effective network - the kind that can lead to a job offer and help you grow and develop as a respected professional in your industry.

However, if you join a professional organization as a job hunter, don't let your enthusiasm and commitment wane after finding a new position. In today's world of downsizings, mergers, global competition and technological change, active membership in a professional organization should be a strategic commitment.

Career-oriented men and women need to learn the arts of asking for what they want, creating win-win, long-term relationships, and establishing a safety net of supportive people who assist each other as resource and referral guides. Active participation in a professional organization is an essential part of this process.

"The difference between what we do and what we are capable of doing would suffice to solve most of the world's problems."

Mohandas K. Gandhi
1869-1948
Indian Independence Leader

Create Your Dream Job, Save the Planet

Steve Howard

29

I gnore the numbers at your own peril. Understand the trends, and prosper in new and green ways. Growing numbers of customers are switching to brands of environment-friendly enterprises. It turns out that what's good for the environment is great for your career. Why? Fewer green products and the jobs that produce them get outsourced to China or India.

Even Wal-Mart decided they couldn't buck the trends. Just ask the head of the newly created sustainability function. While he came from Ernst & Young, he had no previous green experience. But, then who does? Therein lays your career opportunity. With the right mix of passion and transferable skills, you can create your own position.

So, if he can pull it off, why can't you? The Knowledge Labs has unearthed the previously hidden, but growing need for Change-Champion Leaders. What's driving the trend? Like customers, the numbers of job seekers who want to work for green companies have been increasing and point the way to significant career opportunities for those who can lead the parade. Like with any other enterprise-wide change initiative, you can minimize the resistance to your success if you conduct organizational learning pilots – what we call Knowledge Laboratories. Here's what you need to know now to become an up-and-coming Chief Sustainability Officer.

First, the numbers: Point out that ninety percent of Americans are now making efforts in their personal lives to intentionally reduce their impact on the environment. When it comes to securing the trust and loyalty of those current or future customers, explain that they want your company to make changes too. And even better, they will pay more for your products if you hit their hot buttons.

Recent surveys illuminate the key trends. Ninety-three percent conserve energy, 89% recycle, 86% conserve water, and 70% explain the importance of environmental issues to their family and friends. What do the trend-setting consumers shop for? Products with recycled content, 62%; Energy-efficient home improvements, 56%; Cleaning supplies, 48%; Organic or other third-party certified foods/beverages, 24%; Energy-efficient cars, 13%; and Green apparel, 10%.

What motivates them to pay even more for environment-friendly products? Saving money in the long-term, 72%; shopping convenience/readily available, 63%; and the health and welfare of future generations, 63%.

As consumers, what do they expect from brands they buy? 93% of Americans passionately believe that companies have a responsibility to help preserve the environment, 91% say they have a more positive image of a company when it is environmentally responsible, and 85% indicated they would consider switching to another company's products or services because of a company's negative corporate responsibility practices.

Second, remind them that in a Google-enhanced world, negative and positive news is easier to find and travels at warp speed. One of the growing Web 2.0 trends is the advent of ranking, rating, and recommending tools. You've probably encountered them on Amazon when ordering a book. Think of it like an online report card. Talking a green game through slick ads isn't enough anymore. Are you getting As or Fs on the practices that really matter?

Reducing pollution through office and manufacturing operations, 71%; designing products/packaging with more environmentally-friendly contents and minimal packaging, 69%; distributing and transporting products more efficiently, 69%; communicating environmental efforts to consumers and employees so each group can support those efforts, 62%; donating money to environmental causes, 59%; and lobbying for environmentally friendly policies, 57%.

Third, appeal to your current and future employees with the green lens. Whatever you are making, if you can add a green dimension to it -- making it more efficient, healthier and more sustainable for future generations -- you have a product that can't just be made cheaper in India or China. But, you have to figure out how to integrate green into the DNA of your whole business.

Now, here's how you earn your money. You'll have to close the gap between what your customers demand and the current status of environmental support in your culture. If your company is typical, the surveys describe just how big that gap probably is: About half of employed adults (52%) think their company should do more to be environmentally friendly. Only about one in five employed adults (22%) say their company already does enough or too much, while about one in four (26%) are just not sure. What's your company's policy? While about seven in ten employed adults (69%) know that their company has an environmental policy, only about a third (32%) knows what that policy is. For some reason employed men are more likely than their female counterparts to say they know their company's environmental policy (35% men vs. 28% women).

Some things never change. Remind you of anything?

You'd think that by now the change management lessons from all the re-engineering, lean manufacturing, ISO and process improvement programs would sink in. But too many companies relegate sustainability to a function like they did in the quality movement days to the quality department-- a single department -- charged with greening everyone else. At companies across industries, you will find informal leaders and change agents in Investor Relations, Public Relations, Environment, Health and Safety, Facilities, Procurement, Risk Management and other even less likely groups leading the charge.

Don't get me wrong. You may have to convince someone in one of those functions to create a position for you to start out. And you'll want their representatives to join your cross-functional implementation team. But, more often than not, those folks swim upstream within their company's culture. They're not seen as part of the mainstream or part of the company's core mission. Rather they're viewed as nonessential and pushy instigators -- folks who come around to mess up your day by telling you that you need to do things differently in the name of saving the earth. Nobody enjoys doing something just to comply with a new procedure.

Companies who didn't get the best practices memo miss out on the creativity that comes from everyone viewing their jobs, departments, and operations through a green lens. No one knows these opportunities as well as those on the front lines -- the ones who talk to customers, who order supplies, who empty trash bins. They know where there's waste, more efficient ways to do things, and toxic messes that no one's paying attention to.

Consumers and employees are listening and waiting for leadership. Even Wal-Mart got the message and in a surprising tipping point moment, Wal-Mart changed. It brought onboard a Vice President of Sustainability.

Talk about trying to close the gap that rivals the Grand Canyon! Not too long ago the environmentalists wrote Wal-Mart off – or worse yet -- saw it as Darth Vader at the center of the evil empire. By virtue of its relentless globalization and well-known business model, Wal-Mart, they said, would never become a sustainable company in this century.

But, what if it did? Everyone knows that Wal-Mart sells to 90% of American shoppers each and every year. Because the challenge and opportunity is so huge, to pull it off, you'd need to build a network fast and talk to as many environmentalists and sustainability experts as possible. Which is exactly what the new VP did.

However, those experts wanted some answers first, before they took him seriously. What about Wal-Mart's transportation system or its solar program? What is Wal-Mart going to do about carbon emissions policies? Where do they get mentioned in Wal-Mart's quarterly assessment of performance? How serious is top management about integrating sustainability into everyday business decisions?

Tough questions required answers not readily available. They conducted a knowledge laboratory to answer them as a way to figure out what worked best as they learned from their initial experiences. In their change management plan, they decided to appeal to the over a million employees working at Sam's Clubs and Wal-Marts across the US first. If, through training and communications, they reasoned, a critical mass of employees decides to voluntarily start and complete a sustainability diet, then they would become advocates to the almost 130 million shoppers in the US. More customers would take notice and tell their friends and relatives to shop at the new, green Wal-Mart. And so on. And so on.

For Wal-Mart, driving sustainability from the bottom up represented a radical departure from business as usual -- given its reliance on highly detailed procedures. But, there was a method to the high-risk madness. Their strategy wasn't to force everyone onto a crash diet, the equivalent of attempting to lose 50 pounds overnight. Instead, they recommended just taking one small step at a time as part of a plan to change a non-sustainable habit to a new one that met a broad definition of personal sustainability – "having enough for now, while not harming the future."

Let's start off with just two volunteers from each store and we'll see how the experiment goes, the design team concluded. They invited volunteers to a paid retreat at which Wal-Mart's trainers guided discussions about creating personal action plans and wrapped up with a session on how to recruit 10 other volunteers to spread the personal sustainability gospel. Reference guides and DVDs assisted the newly minted sustainability-change-agents when they enrolled the rest of the staff to develop their own plans.

The idea was to change behavior by getting people to change tiny behaviors and achieve early successes. But, not everybody is committed. (Where have we experienced that before?) Some stores have shrugged off the program altogether while in others employees were so enthusiastic that they developed store-level programs and expanded them to local community-wide initiatives.

One store has recycled 8,000 tires, doubled paper and aluminum recycling, and created community teams that include the mayor and the city landfill manager. While still only a drop in the bucket, Wal-Mart is counting on the company's obsession with its core mission, its relentless tracking of results, and its correction of error meetings to continuously improve the results from the first knowledge laboratory.

Lessons learned: What does it take to create a CSO position or as in Wal-Mart's case, a Vice President of Sustainability?

In a word: leadership. Employees hunger for it. Early adopters look to you for permission to do what they're already passionate about. Once you're in your new job, you'll find that you have to wear many hats at once -- an advocate and educator, a visionary, a change manager and a cheerleader, and above all else, a results-driven manager.

CSOs who create these kinds of opportunities feel like an insider with outsider tendencies. Like all leaders who undertake a fundamental reinvention, it's difficult being both. You need to build visibility and support from the top. Wal-Mart's CEO has announced bold, clear goals for the company: to produce zero waste, to use 100% renewable energy, and to supply customers with sustainable products.

Of course it is true that the highest levels of the organization must support the CSO's efforts fully, but it's rare to have that kind of support from the beginning. You'll need both charisma and a compelling message for the organization to want to follow and recognize the practical benefits, both financial and environmental.

You need to build a consensus around what it means to be a sustainable company based on a solid understanding of your organization's culture. Expect a handful of change champions with just as many status quo advocates who may go out of their way to sabotage your initiatives in the name of cost effectiveness and unproven ROI.

Employees, suppliers, customers and investors will range anywhere from grudgingly doing what is required by law to actively driving sustainability principles into business strategy.

Use a change-management consultant to co-design a knowledge laboratory – a low risk, high impact pilot to examine your organization's products, services, processes, and procedures. You can determine the pace and scope of change that best fits your probable adoption rate. You'll have many more questions than answers in the beginning. Learn from your experience and apply what you learn to your next knowledge lab.

Create an environmentally conscious culture by instituting some basic programs. Partner with human resources to recruit and retain green-minded employees and communicate your environmental vision and mission.

Convince them that having a strong environmental ethic can help companies improve business results and they're one of the key players when it comes to hiring, training, enhancing morale and productivity, limiting job turnover, and helping firms increase performance.

Get them involved with learning modules employees can take to improve their knowledge and skills. Seek their facilitation skills when conducting cross-functional green teams that meet regularly to exchange ideas and share new discoveries in carefully designed knowledge laboratories.

Human resources can provide environmental help desks to answer typical employee questions about how to recycle something, where to find green supplies, and the like. They can book a brownbag speaker series all year long, bringing in local and national experts on a range of environmental topics. There's no end to what's possible. The call-to-action is really an opportunity for innovation in product design, packaging, and distribution.

Some of the fundamental questions this process raises will be challenging to address. You won't be able to address all of them at one time, but you better account for them in your long-term change plan.

- Does the company take the full product life-cycle impact into consideration in materials used and energy consumed making, delivering, using and recycling the product?
- Can services be delivered without on site physical presence, thus avoiding service vehicles?
- Are facilities benchmarked against their peers for a truer understanding of efficiency?

- Can employees effectively telecommute a certain percent of the time?
- Can organizations recognize that how they've worked in the past may not reflect how the organization or customer will work in the future?

Pick some low hanging fruit to build high degrees of involvement and early wins. Set up project plans and conduct knowledge laboratories as a way of addressing the more complex and challenging issues after you gain initial momentum.

It is unlikely that as a CSO you will have an organizational structure surrounding your efforts that provides direct power to affect change. But in a sense, that is unimportant. Leadership only occasionally comes from the organization's leaders.

Few organizations today can articulate their sustainability vision. Lots of innocuous feel good statements exist on corporate web pages, but vision is lacking.

For Wal-Mart there are nagging doubts in many quarters about just how sincere that effort is--doubts magnified when Wal-Mart postponed the release of its own long-awaited sustainability progress report.

And that's okay: we're new at this.

But in five years we will go from a small handful with a vision to many hundreds with a vision. The numbers add up in your favor. Get in on the ground floor and you too will prosper in new and green ways. As you'll soon discover, there are many other creative and innovative ways of adapting this to your situation. My hope is that you'll pass on what you learned. Let me know. Together we can spread the word.

"The biggest mistake you can make is to believe that you are working for somebody else. Job security is gone. The driving force of a career must come from the individual. Remember: Jobs are owned by the company, you own your career."

Earl Nightingale
1921-1989
American Radio Announcer,
Author, Motivator, Speaker

Be a Problem Solver

Steve Amos

30

You had better know why you are employed. Your only job security is to be very good at your job and contribute to the company bottom line. This is a how to article on becoming a problem solver so you can improve your career potential.

We all work for one of three reasons:

1. Make money
2. Save money
3. Solve a problem

Employers and customers will pay for services and skills they need. If you contribute more than you cost, you will be hired. It is that simple. So how do you become indispensable?

Propose Solutions

Anyone can find a problem. The truly valuable person solves them. The most value you can offer is to propose (several) possible solutions to solve problems you find. You need to do more than say something is wrong. Figure out possible solutions when you present the problem to your superiors.

213

Define the problem before you look for solutions. Why is it a problem? Who is affected? How are they affected? Poor solutions are the result of skipping this step. A properly defined problem is half solved.

Make a list of all possible causes. Finding what changed is often a quick way to isolate a root cause. Find out if the problem existed before the changes were made. Go deeper and find out what else could have caused your problem.

Look at the problem from different viewpoints. How does the customer see it? How does it affect the suppliers? Call your clients to see if and how the problem may be affecting them. For example, when you have customer service complaints, call your company and see how hard it is for customers to get service.

Talk with other people about ways to solve the problem. Problem solving is often a team effort and we build on other people's ideas. Find experienced coworkers or user groups who may have already solved this problem.

The people who get ahead are the problem solvers, not the problem finders.

Be willing to be blamed.

I often made decisions for groups as a young (22-year-old) engineer because I would take responsibility for making a choice. I did not go off on my own. I had sat through the same meeting and heard the same information as everyone else. I was just willing to summarize our options and verbalize which seemed to be the best path. I was amazed at the relief others showed because I was willing to speak up.

Work 1% more.

Working more and smarter than the competition by just a small amount differentiates you from the masses. The difference at the end of a race often comes from just being a little better. Credit Brian Tracy for promoting this concept. It works wonders.

Know yourself.

Find a career using your best talents. We all have different gifts and skills. Learn what your strengths are and what comes easily to you. What you are passionate about? How can you combine them?

Find at least two or three skills at which you can earn a living. Think about how your skills fit into companies outside your industry. For example, instead of, "I'm a partner at an accounting firm," you could say "I'm a finance professional with in-depth knowledge of the hospitality industry with skills that I could use for hospitals, hotels, retail and other customer-service environments."

Find work that uses your blessings 50% to 80% of the time. No career is perfect. We all have to do tasks we don't like. Not many people enjoy filing expense reports or tax forms. You will be more successful if you use what comes naturally to you than struggle to work at something that pays more.

Know your business.

Know more than just your responsibilities. Know your customers and how they use your products. Know your competitors and their offerings. How are they different, better, or worse?

Look for ways to improve profits, save costs or offer new services. Learn what technologies may help your business. Stay engaged. Find out how you can take advantage of your strengths.

Take action.

Action drives results. Call clients or problem customers. Research new ideas. Plan and write proposals for your business. Do quality work on time. Tackle the projects that make a difference. Start with the harder tasks and get them out of the way.

Take on additional responsibilities.

Be willing to take on special projects, make sure a client is taken care of, make a presentation, organize work to be given to others, and follow up. The problem is often who is going to make something happen. Be the person who gets things done.

Be replaceable.

Organize your work so you can delegate and take on new work. Make the effort to have files and information ready to share. If you are irreplaceable, how can they promote you?

Invest in knowledge and innovation.

I am currently coaching a senior VP in transition who wants to take the best leadership training she can get. She will go to France for the training versus New York because the training in France is better. She says that if the new company won't pay for it, she will. Invest in yourself and in tools that will get you ahead. Diversify your skills.

Be a leader.

Delegation, motivating others to do their best work, taking initiative, thinking strategically, and a positive attitude are all leadership skills that everybody -- even if you are not in a leadership position -- needs to show.

If your workplace is quaking with layoff fears, stand out as someone who stays positive and optimistic. Don't be a Pollyanna and deny what's going on. Acknowledge it and the sadness of seeing colleagues go. But stay positive. That's a leadership quality.

Start to learn how to be a good leader by being a good follower first. Do your part well and learn what everyone around you does. See how everyone contributes. That includes helping to solve problems. "From where you sit, what kind of suggestions do you have for possibly increasing revenues or decreasing expenses?"

Leadership is learned, not just a gift someone has. Anyone can lead by working better and smarter. Try to learn a little more day by day.

Summary
The work world is always changing. Competition and the need for excellent service are always in demand. Do not just get by. Be indispensable, solve problems, and enjoy your work.

"I am not afraid of storms, for I am learning to sail my ship."

Louisa May Alcott
1832-1888
American Author

10 Rules for Growing a Business or Career

31

Janet L. Newcomb & Michael D. Hardesty

When Mike and I met we realized that, although we each had different specialties, we shared very common backgrounds and perspectives. We both have law degrees and we both had big corporation experience. However, neither one of us was currently practicing law. Instead we were both working with small to medium-sized businesses and the executives associated with them. As soon as Mike shared his "10 Rules for Growing a Business" it was clear that these rules were easily translated to an individual's career. So we've done that for you here. It also occurred to us that if you want a successful career, you need to treat it just as seriously as you would a business.

Rule 1 – Plan
- **Business** - Create a strategic plan for growing your business, establish benchmarks for performance, and hold your managers responsible for the numbers.
- **Career** – Create a strategic plan for your career. Determine what you want to achieve and when. Have back-up plans and think about how your skills transfer

to another company or industry. Find someone to hold you accountable for progress toward your goals.

Rule 2 – Be Aware and Adjust

- **Business** - Don't wait for annual reviews to adjust your Business Plan. Markets and competitors don't wait for annual planning reviews, nor should you.
- **Career** – Your yearly performance review is too late to find out that things are changing. The world and the career landscape are currently undergoing enormous upheaval. As problems or opportunities present themselves, be ready to address them.

Rule 3 – Continuously Learn and Develop

- **Business** - Every business owner must make a personal transformation from technical expert to master strategist for the enterprise or find a partner suited to that role and other needed roles.
- **Career** – Understand who you are. Know what you can easily learn and develop and what tasks and careers are best avoided for optimal use of your energy. We're all good at something. **Leverage your strengths and manage your weaknesses. Know and respect the strengths and weaknesses of others.**

Rule 4 – Act in the NOW

- **Business** - Adopt the three cardinal principles of business growth: Drive the numbers higher today; drive the numbers higher tomorrow; and drive the numbers higher this week. If you focus on growing your business in the short run, in a way that's consistent with your vision and values, you won't have to worry about growth over the long run.
- **Career** – Personal growth, personal growth, personal growth. Keep your long term vision in mind, but stay

focused on what you can do today to keep learning and growing. Pay attention to how business needs are shifting and keep your skills up to date. Don't dream about it; do it. There will always be work for someone whose skills match the needs of the marketplace.

Rule 5 – Measure It to Manage It

- **Business** - Develop a financial and operational reporting system that allows you to track your critical numbers. If you don't measure it, you can't manage it.
- **Career** – Budget and save and track your progress. Good financial management will give you the freedom to choose your next job, retire when you want, or pursue a long-term dream.

Rule 6 – Communicate, Communicate, Communicate

- **Business** – Hold a daily management "powwow" with all department heads to go over the numbers and make adjustments to the daily action plans.
- **Career** – Stay in contact with all those who can impact your career, inside and outside the company where you work. Building these connections through regular communication will help if you need their influence.

Rule 7 – Control Costs

- **Business** – Control your costs when growing your business by budgeting percentages rather than dollars. Percentages give you a perspective relative to your peers and competitors. Focusing on dollars is a distorted view. You may be earning at a clip to make $150,000 a year and think you are hot stuff. But if you stay grounded on the percentages versus the absolute dollars, maybe you could earn $250,000!
- **Career** – Control your costs so that you always have a rainy day fund. In an unpredictable business

environment, it makes sense to have at least six months of living expenses tucked away so that you can survive a job hunt and not have to take a job you don't want.

Rule 8 – Identify Key People
- **Business** – Identify all the key people who are driving your business and create incentives for each of them to grow your business for you.
- **Career** – Identify key people who can help grow your career. Some people actually create a board of advisors they can turn to for objective career advice. Create incentives for them to help you by seeing how you can contribute to them first.

Rule 9 – Innovate
- **Business** - Throw out the old management model you started your business with and create a new one. Innovation in management systems is the key to outdistancing your competitors in the race to the top.
- **Career** – Think creatively about how many ways you can achieve your goals. Think creatively about how to reframe your goals, if necessary, in light of changes in the marketplace. Creative and innovative people are the ones that adjust to change most easily - and this is definitely a time of change!

Rule 10 – Play to Win and Enjoy the Game
- **Business** – Growing a business is like competing in a championship sport. Play the way a championship athlete plays: Play to win instead of playing not to lose. And . . . enjoy the game.
- **Career** – Isn't growing a career the same? Play to win, be good at what you do, and have fun! Life is too short to hate your job.

The 7 Habits of a Highly Effective Job Search

John Hall

32

I am a great fan of Steven Covey's remarkable best seller *The Seven Habits of Highly Effective People*, published in 1989 by Simon and Schuster. Covey studied the most successful men and women in the nation and found that they had developed seven habits which distinguished them from their less successful contemporaries. As I read his book, it seemed obvious to me that a job search incorporating Covey's 7 Habits would be "Highly Effective" and candidates would be light years ahead of the competition.

Habit 1: Be Proactive

Most job hunters focus on traditional reactive job techniques such as: attempting to create the perfect resume, an unobtainable goal; focusing too much energy on the published job market, including the Internet; and finally, chasing executive recruiters. Don't get me wrong, all of these things should be part of a well-structured job search, but they should be used in proportion to their probable success. For example a management level job hunter has a 10 percent probability of landing a management position using published resources, including the Internet. The probability of success with recruiters is about five percent. With these statistics in mind, a well structured 40-hour per week job search should devote only four hours a week on the published job market, and two hours contacting recruiters.

The proactive job hunter does not react to the known job market. Rather they look at industry trends and target companies where there are problems that they can solve. They are constantly asking themselves, "Where are my target organizations changing, growing, bleeding, or hurting. What is going on in the industry, in my target companies, where I can present myself as a change agent, where I can demonstrate that I'll bring more value than I'll cost?"

Answering these questions may mean 40 or more hours of intensive library and/or Internet research, supplemented with networking in professional organizations and information interviews with industry leaders. Such proactive approaches quickly distinguish job hunters from 95 percent of their competition, because most job hunters are reactive.

Habit 2: Begin with the End in Mind

Time and again I have seen individuals starting a job search not cognizant about how their next position might add to their overall career growth. Sadly, most men and women think only in terms of their next job, giving little or no consideration to where the next job fits with where they will be in 5, 10, or 20 years. As a result they embark on a job search without considering their values, skills, interests, and long-term career goals. Is it surprising then, that at mid-life millions of individuals are frustrated with their jobs and careers?

One of the most effective ways of beginning with the end in mind is to develop a clear focus on your values, motivated skills, and interests. Once these factors are clearly identified, the next step should be the development of a personal strategic plan, including a mission statement. Steven Covey's "7 Habits" book is an excellent resource to help in developing a personal strategic plan.

Habit 3: Put First Things First

Too many job hunters leap into their search, spending endless hours perfecting their resume, answering ads, and contacting recruiters. Delegated to the back burner are those proactive tasks that should come first, namely research on themselves, their industry, and appropriate companies.

In reality research is the critical first step in a management level job campaign. Nationally respected writer and career expert Tom Jackson feels that research pays off at the rate of $300 per hour. It works this way: If you earned $52,000 per year and you land your next position one week sooner because of your research, you have in effect earned $1,000. If your research helps you land that next position a month sooner you will be over $4,000 ahead. Suppose your research enables you to demonstrate added value, suggest an innovative idea, or present a proposal that increased your initial offer 15 to 20 percent, how much have you earned? Putting First Things First, namely in-depth research, pays very well.

Habit 4: Think Win-Win

Steven Covey stresses that business and personal effectiveness is achieved through cooperation rather than comparisons and competition. Life, he feels, is not a zero-sum game. It pays us to look for the Win-Win Agreement in all our business and personal undertakings. Covey states, "A Win-Win Agreement is an effective tool for establishing the win-win foundations necessary for long-term effectiveness, and may be created between employers and employees..."

Several years before I read *7 Habits,* I had concluded that the most effective tool an executive or manager could use to land a top-level position was a well-written proposal. After reading *7 Habits,* I concluded that a proposal based on Covey's five elements of a Win-Win Agreement would put its author light years ahead of all candidates. Those five elements are:

- **Desired Results:** Identify what is to be done and when.
- **Guidelines:** Specify the parameters within which results are to be accomplished.
- **Resources:** Identify the human, financial, technical, or organizational support available to help accomplish the results.
- **Accountability:** Set up the standards of performance and times for evaluations.
- **Consequences:** Specify--good and bad, natural and logical--what does and what will happen as a result of achieving or not achieving desired results.

Habit 5: Seek First to Understand, Then to Be Understood

Communication is the most important skill for anyone seeking an executive or management level position. The most important communication skill is not speaking, it is listening. Listening is ahead of education, experience, or a perfect resume. In a job interview too many candidates do not listen with the intent to understand; they listen with the intent to reply, make a great impression and get an offer.

Steven Covey stresses empathic listening, listening for an in-depth understanding of the other person's point of view. He feels that without understanding the other person there is little hope that they will understand you. Put another way, people hire people they like, people they feel comfortable with, and whom they feel understand their needs. Once the candidate understands the employer's needs in-depth, he can proceed with the second step of the interaction, seeking to have the employer understand him. Empathic listening helps candidates gather the information necessary to develop proposals.

Habit 6: Synergize

A synergy takes place when the whole is greater than the sum of its parts. One plus one equals 5, 10, or a 100. When I have facilitated brainstorming sessions with a group of five or six outplacement clients I am sometimes overwhelmed by the way they develop ideas for each other. They produce far better results than any of them could alone. Time and time again these brainstorming groups have developed ideas, concepts, and leads that I, the expert who has helped hundreds of corporate executives find jobs, didn't think of. When I see these groups in action I stand back, let them go, and just say WOW to myself.

If you are looking for a job and are not in an outplacement program and/or a support group that utilizes the synergy of group brainstorming, consider forming one. Many churches have support groups.

Habit 7: Sharpen the Saw

Most of us realize that we should upgrade our current skills, learn new skills, exercise regularly, and spiritually renew ourselves. However, we get so busy earning a living, "Sawing," as Steven Covey puts it, that we don't take the time to renew ourselves, or as Covey puts it, we don't take time to "Sharpen the Saw."

Several years ago I had an outplacement client in his mid-fifties who had an undergraduate degree in engineering and an MBA. When he began his search for a new position he quickly learned that his skills were a decade or more out of date. He did not know CAD or TQM. When I asked him why he hadn't kept up to date he said that his company wouldn't let him, which I found extremely difficult to believe. Furthering questions revealed that it was not that his company wouldn't let him, but that they would not pay for the classes and seminars he needed to keep his "Saw" sharp. In effect he was unwilling to pay the price of keeping his "Saw Sharp" during the seventeen years he was with the aerospace company. In the end he paid dearly because he had to spend a year in school to reeducate himself before he could expect to land a comparable position outside the aerospace industry.

We live in a world where change is explosive, a world where mankind's accumulated knowledge is doubling every five years, a world where we need to completely reeducate ourselves every four to six years just to stay even. As a result, we live in a world where homework and continuing education is simply a basic survival skill for career stability. We live in a world where career stability comes not from employment but rather from employability. As you begin to organize your job search it may be a good idea to do an inventory on your professional skills and knowledge. Are they state-of-the-art or do you need to do some "Sharpening of your Saw?"

If you found this discussion of how Steven Covey's 7 Habits of Highly Effective People relates to job search, you might find his book of the same name quite a valuable resource. I also recommend his book First Things First. Both of these books are first class guides for executive and management level job campaigns.

13 Ways to Stay Off the Endangered Species List

33

Steve Howard

Here's the First Secret: There's an 800-pound gorilla in the room. If you are a Baby Boomersaur, according to many of my HR colleagues, you may already be on "The List." I call it the "endangered species list." Nobody in HR will tell you. It's confidential. You are probably making too much money. Chances are you have been with your company for so long that you're clogging the promotional arteries for everybody else who's younger than you. So, at the first excuse – a merger, a couple of missed quarters on Wall Street or a major deal that didn't close – you're on the street going through what we professionals call a career transition.

That's when you discover almost everything you thought you knew about careers and job seeking is wrong. It's not all about resumes and networking. That stuff doesn't work any more. And, here's the irony. Human resources will read between the lines on your resume, detect your age and place you in the stack over there – the out to pasture pile.

But there is good news.

The Second Secret: It's all monkey business, or a barrel of monkeys business, to be more precise. Here is a test. "How

229

many monkeys does it take to remove a boomersaur from the endangered species list?" The answer? One hundred. Why 100 monkeys? The rest of the secrets will help me explain.

The Third Secret: You want the "Hundredth Monkey Effect" working for you. According to Wikipedia, that online encyclopedia, the effect refers to that instant when an idea is spread to the remainder of a population once a certain portion of that population has heard of the new idea or learned the new ability. Wikipedia says, "The story ... apparently originated with Lyall Watson in his 1979 book *Lifetide*. In it he claimed to describe the observations of scientists studying macaques (a type of monkey) on the Japanese island of Koshima in 1952. Some of these monkeys learned to wash sweet potatoes, and gradually this new behavior spread through the younger generation of monkeys in the usual fashion, through observation and repetition."

However, Watson claimed that the researchers observed that once a critical number of monkeys were reached — the so-called hundredth monkey — this previously learned behavior instantly spread across the water to monkeys on nearby islands. We're talking islands separated by great distances of ocean. Imagine if you could harness this in your job search!

The Fourth Secret: How the 100 monkeys approach really works directly challenges the myth of networking. We all know that when you apply networking to your search you are supposed to attend large meetings, talk to as many people as you can, collect their business cards and find the hidden job market. Instead you spend hours in administrative hell logging in everyone's contact information. The more meetings you attend, the farther behind you become – not to mention a little lighter in the wallet.

Here's a better way that I learned from my colleague and friend, John Davies. He wrote a book about his transition from software co-founder to aborted company president to author and eventually to Vice President of Green Research for a research and advisory firm.

Before his publisher changed the title to "The $100,000+ Career," John called it the "Law of 100" and branded himself as a "Co-Conspirator, turning products into profits."

The Fifth Secret: Here's how I save you $20.00. At the heart of his book you won't find networking like you will in almost every other book on the market. John could never bring himself to network even though he was highly sociable and delivered keynote speeches at professional and trade organizations. Instead, you'll find how a chain of introductions gets you the job that fits your passion and is the one for which you are most qualified.

John updated a practice that took place in the 18th century. According to John, when a young man moved from Boston to a brand new city like Philadelphia, he'd carry with him a sealed letter of introduction. With it, written by someone who could vouch for that young person, the newcomer could establish lines of credit at a bank, gain access to influencers in the local society and travel in key circles of commerce.

So John overcame his reluctance to network in the same way, by getting a person he knew well to introduce him to a person they knew well with the goal of reaching 100 introductions. By introduce he meant they would call ahead of time on John's behalf or write an e-mail (composed by John) or invite John and the new person to lunch with the intermediary. He told each of the new people he met in this manner that he was writing a book (which he did) and wanted their advice and perspective. But John would also describe the type of opportunities he was looking for and solicit their advice and ideas for his search.

The Sixth Secret: When John first explained how it worked to me, I imagined that toy game called a "Barrel of Monkeys" – little plastic creatures with outstretched hands that hooked together in interesting chains. The instructions on the bottom of the barrel state, "Dump monkeys onto table. Pick up one monkey by an arm. Hook other arm through a second monkey's arm. Continue making a chain. Your turn is over when a monkey is dropped." To me, that meant it was my responsibility to introduce others to key people as well. It's not just me, me, me.

As John explained the Law of 100 to new introductions, they'd more than likely go along with him and introduce him to another monkey in his chain. At a recent presentation John told us it wasn't uncommon for someone to ask what number he was on – as in 63 out of 100, for instance.

John used the 100 introductions approach to achieve the next step in what he thought was his career progression, the president of a software company in southern California. That was great news. He landed. He proved his thesis. His chain of 100 introductions worked so well and was so novel that his book detailing his adventure was published. But, there was only one thing wrong. John told me he was miserable in an unfulfilling job.

After a little soul searching about why, John began a new round of monkey chains. This time John's journey ended faster, as he had already been involved in this monkey business. He created a brand new position, first as a consultant. He pitched it as a try-before-you-buy arrangement by convincing the CEO of a research and advisory firm to consider a new service offering and together they would figure it out. They did. The CEO agreed John should head it up. And the rest is history, you might say. He moved to Boston and rented out his Newport Beach home. Today, you can receive his "The Green Alert" in your email inbox.

The Seventh Secret: What about boomersaurs on the endangered species list? You started your transition by being on your former organization's list and you can't get hired at a new company because they have their own list. Officially, HR recruiters disavow any age discrimination when it comes to older boomer candidates applying for traditional jobs. But, like the 800-pound gorilla sitting in the room, nobody talks about it and yet everyone knows it goes on - especially HR boomersaur professionals going through their own transition.

The Eighth Secret: Often boomers are shocked when they're laid off. If they've worked for years in one organization, it's easy for them to assume that every organization works the same way. But definitions of marketability and employability changed in the last few years due to outsourcing, globalization, and more mergers and acquisitions. Growth jobs require intimate familiarity with all things Internet -- Web 2.0 and the kinds of technology that only boomersaur's children (and in some cases, grandchildren) take to so effortlessly and loudly -- iPods, Blogs, instant messaging, social networks – stuff that old dogs find difficult to learn. So, slow-learning boomersaurs end up stuck in a tar pit or are put out to pasture somewhere while they call back, "Hey, wait a minute, I used to be somebody. Dammit!"

The Ninth Secret: What can boomersaurs do? I recommend finding an emerging industry. How? Look for a convergence of forces. It happens once, or maybe twice, in a career if you are lucky. In John's case, he noticed how big business and investors saw profit reasons for becoming greener, rather than just political or social responsibility reasons. It took a while, he told me, just to figure out how to monetize the trends in a way that would provide a job for him. But he did, and so can you. How many monkeys? One hundred; just checking.

One way is to find out what investors favor. They place bets over three to five-year windows. The top three industries venture capital firms invested in for 2006 were Life Sciences, Web 2.0 and Alternative Energy. Sure, many of these individual investments won't work out. However by 2011 these industry niches will be well on their way to becoming rapid growth forces in the marketplace. Let's stay with green, as John did, as an example.

How would you go about supporting yourself with the growth opportunities in green? First, you need to look inside yourself and figure out whether you have a personal passion. Remember John's mistake? Let's say you have the passion and you're an entrepreneur wanting to identify new business opportunities, or maybe you're a new college graduate without any work experience or a seasoned veteran with no experience in the emerging green niche – like John.

How do you take advantage of the opportunity? The good news is hardly anyone else knows more or has more experience in a newly emerging niche. If they do, enroll them in your informal advisory board to share knowledge and experience. Ask one of your 100 monkeys for an introduction.

The Tenth Secret: To find your niche, it's best to stay within your prior expertise whenever possible. You're looking for an angle. For the new grad, how can you link your iTunes, iPod, podcasting, digital video, and social networking skills – MySpace, YouTube or Facebook -- with the green opportunities? Is it working for a skateboarding and clothing manufacturer who is appealing to your age group with organic-only materials and renewable components?

If you're a seasoned boomersaur, how can you apply your marketing and advertising expertise? If you've honed your skills in investor relations, public relations, environment, health and safety, facilities, procurement, or risk management over your career, you'll have an easier time creating a job to focus on green initiatives, since these are the functions already driving green improvement programs in other companies. How about your financial or manufacturing experience? Do you have engineering expertise or human resources talents? Or, what if you possess supply chain software experience, like John?

Have you championed ISO or continuous improvement initiatives? You might have a leg up based on your experience since, when fully implemented, green sustainability systems evaluate all of the organization's products, services, processes, procedures and business practices.

The Eleventh Secret: How else can you find the right fit? Read the headlines to figure out some clues. It used to be that every April – before and after Earth Day – newspapers, magazines, and television news programs examined the debate about global warming – and then moved on to other topics. But, in 2007 and in the successive months, it has become increasingly difficult to avoid an ad, an article, or a documentary describing almost every green thing imaginable. If you live in the West, west of the Rockies that is, then chances are your state government has earmarked grants, tax incentives and regulations to curb emissions. Small businesses usually can find favorable treatment when applying for funds. Ask your 100 monkeys for introductions.

Understand the markets for clean technology, renewable energy, community efforts to clean up the environment, and promotions of toxic-free products and packaging. Entrepreneurs shouldn't lack for ideas. Problems and opportunities include implications of weather changes, ethanol production that drives up the price of corn, hybrid vehicles vs. auto industry resistance to emission targets, carbon-trading credits, alternative energy investments, community events, citizen conservation tips, home builder LEED certification and surveys tracking what consumers by every segment believe about the companies and products they buy from them.

Subscribe to trade magazines and consider becoming a thought leader by publishing your own newsletter or blog. Remember, in five years we will go from a small handful of green monkeys with a vision to many hundreds of green organizations with a vision and best practices. Even human resource groups can contribute in their organizations by articulating visions and driving them into their organizations. Early adopter companies will have the influence to drive innovation that truly will transform their respective industries and attract the talent they want away from their competitors.

The Twelfth Secret: Keep up with market analysis and changing customer attitudes. For instance Cone Consumer Environmental Survey in 2007 reported that 93% of Americans believe companies have a responsibility to help preserve the environment.

Solid majorities support meaningful company actions including:

- Reducing pollution through office and manufacturing operations- 71%
- Designing packaging with more environmentally friendly contents and minimal packaging- 69%
- Distributing and transporting products more efficiently- 69%
- Communicating environmental efforts to consumers and employees so each group can support those efforts- 62%
- Donating money to environmental causes- 59%
- Lobbying for environmentally-friendly policies- 57%

The Thirteenth Secret: Another way to find business opportunities is partnering with complementary firms or consultants. Consider asking for introductions to other entrepreneurs already operating in this arena.

Before you get stuck, subscribe to my blog. Join my Barrel of 100 Monkeys and you can find each other, one green monkey at a time. Since this is about the environment, be sure to pick up after yourself. Don't leave those banana peels on the ground. Somebody could get hurt.

Lost in Translation

34

Janet L. Newcomb & Krystal Jalene Thomas

Leaders say they can't find good people. Good people complain that they can't find jobs. What is going on? We talked to executives, human resource professionals, recruiters and job seekers, and learned that each player in the talent game has different perspectives and different needs. The fast pace of the race to find good people often impedes effective communication. The resulting confusion leaves good people lost in translation. Here's what everyone is really saying:

Executives define "good people" as those with skill and personality.

Leaders assess candidates based on two key criteria: (1) Aptitude - does an employee have the ability to execute and (2) Attitude - will he/she be a good fit on the team?

"Degrees and theoretical knowledge are a given," remarked a technology executive, "but I'm looking for problem solvers—people with experience that I can trust to make good sound judgments and deliver results."

Although every manager is different, most leaders want someone who can hit the ground running and get things done.

237

"The work-a-day world is busy," said an apparel executive. "I'm constantly getting more responsibility for my division and my team. When I'm interviewing someone, I'm searching for what else they can take off my plate."

In the leaner world of nimble organizations, a candidate who is a jack of all trades and master of a few is valued. People that are flexible, adaptable and capable give leaders more options. "I interviewed a candidate that didn't have the exact skill I needed, but had other skills we didn't have on the team. I knew the time it would take to train her in that one skill would be a small investment in exchange for what she would bring to the team."

And speaking of motivation, it's not just about what an employee can do, but how they do it. "As many hours as we work, the real goal is to like the people we work with," said an entertainment executive. "If the personalities don't mesh, the work just won't get done right. Our motto is the drama belongs in the script, not in the break room."

Executives want good people, NOW!

Leaders have little patience for or understanding of the recruiting and hiring processes that may be required to satisfy legal requirements.

"My need is usually immediate. It's often easier for me to go into my network, get someone I know and be done with it, rather than wait four weeks for the process to identify someone I don't know," commented one source. This urgency often leads executives to communicate sparsely about their needs. They often assume you understand what they want, even if they haven't clearly communicated that to you.

Human Resource Professionals have more to do than just recruit good people.

When recruiting, HR professionals are concerned primarily with (1) meeting the organization's need for high quality talent in a timely and cost-effective manner and (2) managing an effective hiring process that satisfies EEO and other legal requirements.

"Our main job is people management and we are good at it," commented one HR source, "but recruitment is only one part of our job. We are also responsible for retaining, training, developing, reporting on, and resolving challenges for the staff already in place. HR is a business in itself."

The focus on HR business often keeps them from learning the business needs elsewhere in the organization, leaving HR professionals at a disadvantage when it comes to sourcing and identifying appropriate talent.

"That's why it's so important for us to be connected in a significant way to the business unit structurally," stated an HR executive, "My HR managers need to partner with division leaders so they become entrenched in the culture and the process of the entire business."

As the middle man, HR can only do so much with the tools they have.
Caught in the middle, HR often feels they are the least empowered to make decisions about talent acquisition. Especially in large organizations, structures which emphasize job listings, career ladders and computer matching may inadvertently screen out good people who don't fit pre-determined categories.

Without exact credentials or previous job titles to guide them, HR may find it difficult to translate a job seeker's resume that has not been tailored to a specific job listing.

"I wish I had those hours in the day for informational interviews where I could really assess people's capability and fit, but I don't," lamented another HR executive. "And on that rare occasion when I do and find someone great, there's often no opportunity to create a place for them inside the company."

Recruiters want direct access to executives.

"I want to hear it from the executive," commented one external recruiter, "not HR because if the two parties aren't aligned, we'll get it wrong. And worse, we'll ruin the relationship with the candidate we've brought to the table."

External recruiters are proactive and results oriented, since without results they don't get paid. They want to bring good people, who may not be an exact fit with the stated requirement, to an executive's attention. "I also want the feedback from executives about their meeting because that helps me think about where else that candidate could fit inside the organization or in another organization."

The lack of direct access can also affect negotiations to close a candidate for a job. "Being upfront with everyone is key," said a high powered entertainment recruiter. "If the candidate has requirements, or the company has specifics, then the sooner we get information on the table, the better for everyone to get things worked out. Our job is to bring both sides into alignment. Third parties can impede that process."

Good people are working and networking.

It's a dog-eat-dog world. Good people are hard to find because the best ones aren't necessarily on the job market. Through networking in multiple industries, recruiters can discover talent that may never look at job listings.

"The perception is that you can't keep a good person down. But the reality is, people make choices, life just happens, and organizational realignments are frequent. Good people, however, will make it a point to find you and be where you are," said a recruiter. "They understand that it's about relationships, not just resumes."

Job seekers want the job *and* personal empowerment.

Yes, job seekers need a job! However, rather than following a traditional career ladder, employees today are looking for growth opportunities. Although long-term employees may see the new workforce as possessing unrealistic expectations, gone are the days of lifetime employment and dependency on one organization. The new contract is based on mutual investment.

"It's pretty simple. I want to be paid fairly for what I do, empowered to do my job and treated as a human being with a life," said one job seeker. "I don't want to be set-up for failure by misaligned expectations."

The new generation wants to know about your culture, how decisions get made, how they will fit into the overall picture and what personal choices the company will honor. Today's employee values time and personal flexibility, in some cases even more than money. And this generation isn't afraid to challenge jobs with great responsibility but little authority or respect.

Job seekers have to cater to everyone in the process—and they often have the least information and access.

"It takes so much stamina to find a job—with so many people in the process to market yourself to. You never know how you are going to be seen and whose need you have to serve to get the real deal about the job." And for many, the process starts with job postings and listings that are already well along in the process of being filled – definitely a dead-end road.

"In my industry, my biggest competition is the internal candidate. I called to follow up on one listing I saw, and the executive mentioned that he'd already decided to promote his assistant. It was a frustrating waste of my time."

More than anything, job seekers want to break through the process and find a great fit. "I want the truth," declared one job seeker. "The worst thing is to interview and be left hanging. It's tough to know how to interpret the silence, but if you let me know what you want, and I tell you what I need, then we can both make decisions about what's going to work."

Tips for Success
Don't assume that you know what the other party wants.

Listen. Ask questions. Probe for details. Be consistent in what you say to everyone. Set clear expectations. Misunderstandings happen when information is repeated differently. It's a good sign when you hear the same information more than once from more than one source. Seek first to understand, and then be understood.

Needs Drive the Recruiting Process

State what you need. What do you want in a boss? In an employee? What's a deal breaker? Without this information, good matches can't be made.

The process doesn't usually allow for a direct sale.

Job seekers have to take the lead in packaging themselves for a job. Tailor the resume. Create your career story. Connect the dots and show how your skills fit the job at hand. If you don't empower the HR person to sell you effectively, you'll likely never get to the executive.

Know the business you want to be in.

Learn the pace, culture, structure, ways decisions get made, and type of people that are successful at the company you are interested in. The internet is a great place to start; but the most overlooked resource is folks who have worked there and can share their experience to complement what's in print.

Good people attract good people.

Be where good people are: networking, parties, trade organizations, conferences, and events. It's all about building relationships and letting people know your needs. Most folks are willing to help, especially if they know who you are.

Conclusion

Talent acquisition is complex. An effective process requires the cooperation of all stakeholders and integration with an organization's larger talent management system.

Acquisition starts with careful analysis of the organization's needs – both current and future projections. It's critical to empower everyone to think more broadly about options to find and place good people. Once requirements are clearly identified, determine together where to locate the desired talent.

And once a good person is found, move quickly to bring them on board. If you find a good person that's not right for your team, let others know that you've found a great person! Keep the lines of communication open. Job seekers must educate themselves, network incessantly and leave nothing to chance!

Good people don't fit into traditional boxes. That's why many are lost in translation.

"You know you are on the road to success if you would do your job and not be paid for it."

Oprah Winfrey
1954-
American Television Host

Meet the Authors

Steve Amos

Steve Amos makes you wonder what he has not done. He is an engineer with diverse experience, a project manager, business owner, speaker, author, marketer, real estate appraiser and investor. Steve helps **Turn Visions into Profits** in new product development, manufacturing, process development and project management. His background is a diverse, productive and an unparalleled education in how business really works coming from hands on work, success and failure.

Steve's experience includes Pentair Water, Goldrush Realty Advisors, Black and Decker, Sargent Lock, Colt Firearms, UNC Resources, United Technologies, Eastman Kodak and several small entrepreneurial companies you never heard of. Products include consumer products, architectural hardware, aerospace turbines, military firearms, nuclear power plants and real estate.

Steve Amos grew up in Henrietta, NY (suburb of Rochester), was educated by the State University of New York at Buffalo, Hartford Graduate Center, hard knocks, and too many training courses to mention. While he has lived in Connecticut, New York, Nevada, and Texas, Steve and his wife currently reside in Aliso Viejo, California.

Steve is avid supporter of Career Builder's fellowship at Crystal Cathedral and Catholic-Christian career groups in Orange County. He speaks on problem solving and careers at businesses, conferences, colleges and churches.

Steve can be reached at (949) 510-6985 or email adaptandthrive@gmail.com. See www.engineeringprofit.com for more information.

Charlotte Backman

After completing a degree in English at UCLA, Charlotte's career "paths" included advertising, administrative positions at Hewlett-Packard, massage therapy, and working with her Dad in construction.

She started to paint rocks, way back when that was a craze in elementary school. After a discouraging high school art class, her creative urges were satisfied with ceramics and beading for quite some time. She began painting in her 40's, and then took up teaching art as well, finally discovering what she wanted to be when she grew up.

Now Charlotte's art is in international collections, including a Hilton Hotel and several spiritual centers in the US. Charlotte's artwork has been published in a unique artistic collaboration with Kathe Schaaf, author of *Some Things I Know to be True,* 2006, the first in a narrative series of six poetry books. She teaches privately and gives workshops internationally.

Visit her interactive website at www.mandalavisions.com.

Rochelle Burgess

Rochelle Burgess is the founder of Innovative Partners in Leadership, Inc. As a Human Resources consultant and coach, she enables her clients to be more effective on the "people side of the business" so that they can enhance their energy in achieving the business results they want. A recognized authority in both Organizational Development and Human Resources, Rochelle has over thirty years of Fortune 500 experience specializing in employee selection and retention, team building, employee relations, training programs, performance management and leadership development.

Rochelle is known for partnering with her clients to create a work environment of high performance standards, continuous professional growth and the desired business results. She customizes workshops to meet the needs of their employees. She conducts employee climate interviews and surveys that result in tangible recommendations with measurable results.

As a faculty member at Chapman University, Rochelle develops and facilitates classes in the Organizational Leadership degree program.

She is currently pursuing a doctorate degree, with a dissertation on the mix of four age generations in the workplace and specifically, communications between Gen-X and Gen-Y. She has often been a keynote speaker and workshop facilitator on this topic and other leadership related issues for Engineering, Executive Outsourcing, Business, University and HR organizations.

She can be contacted at (949) 439-3214, or via e-mail at RSBurgess@Innovative-Partners.org.

John Hall

John Hall has coached hundreds of executives and management employees through career transitions. At Chapman University, he developed and taught the only graduate outplacement course in the nation. He also taught *Advanced Job Search Strategies* in the Graduate Career Counseling Program at the University of California, San Diego.

John has had articles published in *The Wall Street Journal's National Business Employment Weekly*, *The Alumni Newsletter for the Wharton Business School* and *the Orange County Register*. For two and one-half years, he hosted a talk show, *Career Strategies* on Talk2K.com. John served three years on the National Board of the Professional Coaches and Mentors Association and is a Past President of their Orange County Chapter. He is currently on the board of the International Coaches Federation's Orange County Chapter.

John is a Past Division Governor in Toastmasters International and Past President of the Los Angeles Area National Speakers Association where he won their Golden Microphone Award. This presentation training and experience has helped him develop an enthusiastic and highly interactive teaching style.

To contact John, call him at (949) 387-2004, email him at john@advancedcareerstrategies.com, or go to his website at www.advancedcareerstrategies.com.

Michael D. Hardesty

Mike Hardesty brings an extensive business background, in addition to a law degree and an MBA, to assist his clients. His many assignments include: corporate troubleshooter in one of the world's largest apparel companies; in-house counsel and advisor to the president; management consultant helping Fortune 500 companies increase productivity and reduce labor costs; owner of his own management consulting firm with offices in Australia, New Zealand, South Africa and the U.S.; mergers and acquisitions, exclusively of law firms; and management consultant helping small to mid-sized firms survive and prosper.

Mike has assisted in the salvation, growth, merger and sale of more than 800 domestic and international companies, both large and small. His analytical ability, no nonsense persona and extensive hands-on experience make Mike the ideal point man to assist anyone thinking seriously about the future of their business.

Mike is currently the managing partner of Hardesty Hackett & Partners, Atlanta, Georgia.

If you are ready for a straight-talking assessment and analysis of your operations, contact Mike at 770-594-1200, mdh@hardestyhackett.com, or www.hardestyhackett.com.

Hal Hendrix

Hal Hendrix combines thirty years of experience in the corporate world with coaching and psychology to create a unique and effective business advisory practice. Hal provides executive coaching to further develop or fine tune specific skill sets, improve performance, expand abilities necessary for the next level of job responsibilities, change corporate culture, and enhance leadership abilities.

His corporate experience, the most recent as CFO and senior management team member, included responsibility for accounting, finance, information systems, strategic planning, inventory and indirect impact on manufacturing management. This background enables him to understand complex business issues, including bottom line impact.

In addition to his broad functional experience, Hal has industry experience in oil and gas, food manufacturing and transportation.

Hal is on the advisory board of Chapman University and played a key role in the curriculum design and development of their Business and Organizational Coaching Certification program. As adjunct faculty, Hal teaches classes in leadership and business coaching certificate programs at both Chapman and San Diego State University.

He received an undergraduate degree in accounting from the University of Tulsa, studied in the MBA program at Loyola College and received an MA in psychology from the University of Santa Monica in 1995. He became credentialed as a Certified Public Accountant in 1973 and a Certified Professional Coach in 2001.

Steve Howard

Steve published the *Journal of 2020 Foresight* and founded The Knowledge Labs as the *authoritative source for the people, places, ideas, trends and the know-how you need to know now.* Today, he conducts four *Best Fit, Best Place Labs* focusing on how to: master the challenges facing all baby boomers; follow your passion to work and live anywhere you want; take advantage of the green revolution; and turn your hobby into a *KnowledgeATM* .

In addition to directing The Knowledge Labs, Steve enjoys coaching freshly minted Executive MBA graduates from the Paul Merage School of Business at UCI as they pursue *career, entrepreneurial and intrapreneurial opportunities.*

Previously, Steve coached hundreds of C-Suite and key executives during their career transitions as Senior Vice President at Right Management Consultants. He held senior management positions at Fluor, Unisys, Western Digital, Proxima and Wyle Electronics.

Steve earned a Masters degree from the Ball State University in Psychology. He is past President of the Orange County Chapter of the ASTD.

You can reach Steve at (949) 292-9502 or at knowlabs@cox.net for information about the latest reports from the *Innovation G-Spots, MobileKnowCo* or *High Country Eagle* labs. And to find out how we're *doing our small part to keep boomersaurs off the endangered species list* visit www.boomersaur.com.

Joanna Maxwell

Joanna Maxwell has found her square hole(s) as a corporate trainer, professional coach and journalist. Her qualifications include ICF coaching accreditation, qualifications in workplace training, a B.A. and an L.L.M. (A Masters of Arts in Journalism is a work-in-progress.)

Round holes she has fallen into along the way include lawyer, life skills teacher, therapist, childcare worker, academic, creative consultant, film writer, barmaid, market researcher and general dogs body. She has also walked on fire, climbed Mount Kilimanjaro and travelled through the Middle East, India, Africa, Asia and Tibet.

Joanna runs career change programs for individuals who are sick of hanging up half their personality with their jackets when they arrive at work each day and are ready to create a genuinely compelling and satisfying career. She also teaches creative thinking to organizations that are ready to think about things in a different way, to find creative solutions for problems, and to give their staff the tools to do their work efficiently and with flair.

Contact Joanna in Australia at 0421-310-370, Joanna@workincolour.com.au or www.workincolour.com.au

Janet L. Newcomb

Jan is a coach and consultant specializing in business leadership and strategy, organizational effectiveness and career transitions. In her 25+ years of wide-ranging business experience, she has worked for Fortune 500 companies, founded for-profit and non-profit corporations, served on the boards of several professional organizations, and is currently an entrepreneur/business owner and community volunteer. In addition to advanced studies in organizational management, Jan holds degrees in sociology and law, as well as certificates in career transition coaching, parent coaching, personal/organizational coaching, mediation, diversity and HR development.

Individuals Jan works with learn to improve personal/organizational results by clarifying and focusing on strengths, identifying blind spots, and managing weaknesses effectively. Her mediation experience makes her particularly effective working with the conflicting priorities and personalities on executive teams. An imaginative thinker who reads widely to stay connected to current market trends, she can help you identify shifting needs and capitalize on emerging opportunities. She particularly enjoys the challenge of working with fast-paced executives learning to enhance their effectiveness while leading more authentic and balanced lives.

Contact Jan in Orange County, California, at 714-847-8933, jasnet714@aol.com or www.focusedcoach.com

Lee Pound

Lee specializes in editing and publishing books for consultants, coaches and other professionals who want to become the recognized experts in their markets. He is also the co-producer of the Speak Your Way to Wealth seminars presented each August in Southern California.

He is the author of seven books, including *57 Steps to Better Writing*, and *Coaching for the New Century*. He has written two novels and three family histories. His publishing company, Solutions Press, specializes in business publications.

Lee started his career as a newspaper editor at the News-Times Newspapers in Placentia, California and later with the Newport Ensign in Newport Beach, California. He was also a chief financial officer in newspaper and magazine publishing for over 20 years.

He started speaking professionally in 1974. In the late 1980's he studied creative writing with Sol Stein, one of the premier book editors of the 20th Century. This led directly to the writing of his novels and to his becoming a writing coach and book publisher.

He is a member of Professional Coaches and Mentors Association, International Coach Federation, Toastmasters International and National Speakers Association.

Lee currently lives in Irvine, California. He can be reached at 949-246-8580. His web sites are www.leepound.com and www.speakyourwaytowealth.com. His email address is lee@leepound.com.

James Richards

James Richards resides in California and has been married to his wife and business partner, Yvonne for 44 years. They have 3 grown sons and 3 grandsons.

James was born and educated in New Zealand and received his Tertiary education at the Auckland Institute of Technology and Harvard Business School in Boston. He built an international printing and publishing business, based in New Zealand and with operations in Australia and the United States.

He was a founding member of the Young Presidents Organization in New Zealand.

Currently he is the President of an Internet business - InterGreet.com, the exclusive online wholesaler of American Greetings products to retail stores and businesses.

He is an ordained Pastor at the Crystal Cathedral in Garden Grove, California where he heads an Outreach Ministry to Third World countries and teaches advanced classes in Biblical Studies. He is the author of the popular Theology book, "100 Questions & Answers".

Recently he launched a cutting-edge Online Seminary and Internet-based English language program for South Asian men and women who he is training to be leaders of the future.

You can contact James at:
E-mail: PastorJames@NewHorizonsMissions.com
Web site: http://www.NewHorizonsMissions.com.
Or
E-mail: JamesR@InterGreet.com
Web site: http://www.InterGreet.com

Jacqueline A. Soares

Jacqueline is the President of Lighthouse Inspirations, Inc. a family of companies and an inspirational incubator for new businesses. The entrepreneur's entrepreneur, she has founded, developed and managed a number of businesses: housekeeping services, custom lampshade design, home decor boutique, family mediation, legal document preparation, wedding officiant (www.Idotoday.com), house sitting services, and credit restoration (www.SCRnow.com) - all while raising and mentoring four children and five grandchildren. Jacqueline knows what it takes to build a successful and profitable business and has experienced it all - from initial concept and struggling start-up, to full-service and profitable reality. She is an inspirational speaker and wise advisor who thoroughly understands the daily challenges entrepreneurs face.

In addition to her wide-ranging business experience and education in both liberal arts and sociology, Jacqueline is an ordained pastor with certificates in paralegal, parenting and mediation.

Contact Jacqueline in Orange County, California, at 714-625-7841, lhi@verizon.net or www.focusedcoach.com

Krystal Jalene Thomas

Krystal Jalene Thomas is an award winning television, web and new media producer. Through her banner Pooka Ventures, she serves as a creative producer and strategic consultant to television, new media and Fortune 500 brands that drive entertainment. With over a decade of experience, her rare combination of creative talent and business savvy has benefited companies such as Disney, Showtime, PBS, and BMW.

The former IBM Organizational Change Consultant has also been a long time advocate in the effort to better lives in the workplace. Today, Krystal works one on one with individuals in career transition to help identify new professional goals and create action plans to realize dreams. A recent career transplant herself, she intimately understands the benefits of life coaching and what it takes to implement a new work-life paradigm.

Krystal holds an MFA from the Peter Stark Producing Program at the USC School of Cinematic Arts and degrees from the Haas School of Business at the University of California, Berkeley.

Contact Krystal in Orange Co., California, at 714-227-0339, kthomas@pookaventures.com or www.pookaventures.com